Stoker, Robert
    Phillip, 1954-

Reluctant partners.

$49.95

DATE			

Pitt Series in
Policy and Institutional Studies

Reluctant Partners

*Implementing
Federal Policy*

ROBERT P. STOKER

UNIVERSITY OF PITTSBURGH PRESS

Published by the University of Pittsburgh Press, Pittsburgh, Pa. 15260
Copyright © 1991, University of Pittsburgh Press
All rights reserved
Eurospan, London
Manufactured in the United States of America

Library of Congress Cataloging-in-Publication Data

Stoker, Robert Philip, 1954–
Reluctant partners : implementing federal policy / Robert P. Stoker.
p.   cm. — (Pitt series in policy and institutional studies)
Includes bibliographical references (p.   ) and index.
ISBN 0-8229-3688-7 (cl)
1. Federal government—United States.   2. Authority.   3. United States—Economic
policy—1945– —Decision-making.   4. Capitalism—United States.   I. Title.
II. Series.
JK325.S79   1991
321.02'0973—dc20   91-50112
                                                                                                              CIP

A CIP catalogue record for this book is available from the British Library.

FOR PATRICIA

DISCARDED

CONTENTS

LIST OF FIGURES   ix

LIST OF TABLES   xi

PREFACE   xiii

1. The Implementation Paradox   3
2. Authority, Exchange, and Governance   20
3. Implementation Regimes   52
4. The Politics of Implementation Regimes   90
5. Policy Reform and Implementation Performance   127
6. Not in My Backyard   152
7. Meeting the Challenge   177

NOTES   191

BIBLIOGRAPHY   201

INDEX   209

FIGURES

1. Reciprocal Decision Making in the
   Implementation Process   38
2. Dollar Division Game   63
3. Dollar Division Game, Graphic Form   64
4. Prisoner's Dilemma Game   65
5. Stag Hunt Game   69
6. Chicken Game   71
7. World/EDA Game   76
8. Dynamics of Regime Change Over Time   85
9. Implementation Regime Typology   95
10. Federalist Regime Design   102
11. Dimensions of Public/Private Choice   118
12. Evolution of the NSLP   131
13. School Participation in NSLP   144
14. Student Participation in NSLP   145
15. Percent Student Participation in NSLP   146
16. Percent Free and Reduced Price Participation   148
17. Prisoner's Dilemma for Low-Level Waste   162
18. Deadlock (at Best) in High-Level Waste   172

TABLES

1. NSLP Participation Over Time   133
2. Federal Grants to NSLP   135
3. Percentage of Free and Reduced Price Participants   136
4. Changes in NSLP Performance   147
5. Low-Level Waste, 1987   160

PREFACE

THIS BOOK is about the supposed disability of the U.S. government. Evidence of disability abounds. Problems, such as poverty, the poor quality of education, and homelessness, seem to defy solution. The list of hapless government programs grows. Policy innovation is constrained by deficit-induced gridlock; the popular press asks, "Is Government Dead?" (*Time*, 10/23/89). My view is that the disability of U.S. government has been exaggerated by journalists and scholars alike. However, the ways in which we think about government and the accomplishment of policy objectives must change if we are to discover a constructive path for national governance.

Scholarly research on the implementation problem has contributed to the view that the U.S. government is disabled. The supposed cause of disability is diffuse authority—the existence of numerous, autonomous participants within the implementation process. In our government, diffuse authority is an important value related to the constitutional principles of liberalism and federalism. But diffuse authority challenges national leadership by placing control of policy-relevant resources in many hands. In this context, the implementation of national policy often depends upon the cooperation of authorities who may be in conflict with the policy's ends or means.

Early implementation research paints a picture of governmental ineptitude; the horrors of the implementation process seem to be exceeded only by the blindness of those who continue to believe that government can be a constructive force in society. This view is an interpretation of the effect of diffuse authority within two influential models of social organization: hierarchies and markets. Classical models of hierarchy emphasize control and coherence, viewing bureaucracy as an ideal model of organization. Diffuse authority, though valued in the U.S. system of political economy, is inconsistent with bureaucracy because it undermines the organization's control system. From a market-oriented perspective, the preferences of implementation participants are constraints that must be satisfied. This view empowers implementors and challenges the legitimacy of political power within representative democracy, as the purposes of the policy formulators are sacrificed to the interests of the implementors.

The emphasis of this book is upon the constitutional principles that divide authority in U.S. government and the implications of this division for governmental effectiveness. A condition of diffuse authority certainly creates a challenging context for policy makers to exercise leadership, but not one which is well understood by conventional interpretations of the implementation problem or the imperatives of government. The key misconception that exists in the literature is that the likelihood of cooperation is inseparable from the intensity of conflict of interest. An implication of this misconception is that cooperation from implementors is unlikely whenever conflict exists over the objectives of national policy. In response, one must either suppress conflict (through comprehensive control of the implementation process) or surrender control of policy (through accommodation of implementors' interests, creating anemic policy) in order to realize cooperation. However, if cooperation is separated conceptually from conflicts of interest—if cooperation is a possible response to these conflicts—the problem for national leaders is to arrange the implementation process so that cooperation is more likely. Focusing on cooperation, policy makers consider the strategic and institutional means by which the actions of independent authorities may be coordinated. This I have called the regime approach to implementation analysis.

A key supposition of this work is that the federal government can contribute to improving social conditions. Government is not the problem, the problem is to govern effectively. In the United States, effective government cannot be based exclusively upon the wisdom of the federal government, but neither can it sacrifice federal leadership. The structure of U.S. government demands that state and local governments and key elements of the private sector be engaged as partners in the implementation of national policy. The central concern of this book deals with how to arrange constructive partnerships to engage the effectiveness of implementors without sacrificing federal leadership. By accomplishing this we may yet realize the full effectiveness of our government.

I have drawn from many sources to develop my ideas about the nature of the implementation problem. However, the work of four others has been especially important to me: Clarence Stone's (1989) work on the nature of political power in urban regimes; F. A. Hayek's (1960) work on liberty and authority; Robert Axelrod's (1984) work on cooperation theory; and Vincent Ostrom's (1987) analysis of the Constitution of the United States and its administrative consequences. I have often drawn insights and inspiration from these sources.

In addition to inspiring me with his work, Clarence Stone was an active participant in the development of this manuscript. He read early drafts of chapters, encouraged me, and helped me to develop my ideas. Since that period more than ten years ago when we studied the field of implementation analysis together, he has been generous with his time and insights. His significant contributions to this work are deeply appreciated.

I also wish to acknowledge my colleagues who supported this effort. At The George Washington University, this research was supported by grants from the Columbian College and the Graduate Institute for Public Policy Research. Several members of my department contributed directly or indirectly to the successful completion of this work. I am grateful to Hugh LeBlanc and Bernard Reich for their support. I am also grateful to those colleagues (especially Jeffrey Henig) who read drafts of material and provided useful comments.

Finally, I could not have completed this work without the love and encouragement of my family. For their support and understanding, I am forever grateful.

Reluctant Partners

1 THE IMPLEMENTATION PARADOX

$\mathbf{A}$N ENDURING challenge for national governance is found in the principles of the political and economic organization of the United States: How is it possible to bring about leadership in a condition of diffuse authority?

A federal polity with a liberal political economy divides authority in two important ways, between market and state and within the structure of the state itself. In the public sector, authority is divided between the federal government and its constituent states. Commercial organization, though operating in a context created and supported by government, is a distinct sector of authority controlling vast resources (on the role of authority in commerce, see Lindblom, 1977).

This diffusion of authority reflects constitutional values at the core of U.S. government. Federalism diffuses authority in government as a protection against the possible excesses of national government and to make national policy initiatives more attuned to local variation. Liberalism—market-oriented economic organization—values diffuse authority in commerce as a condition required to enjoy the innovation and efficiency of markets. However, a diffuse distribution of authority also has the effect of placing many policy-relevant resources beyond the direct control of federal officials, challenging their ability to achieve national policy goals.

To implement policy the federal government must often solicit cooperation from other authorities. If national leadership is nominal, or if it merely reflects the preferences of other authorities, willing partners are easily found to implement federal policy. However, those who "help" to implement federal policy may not always be inclined to agree with its purposes or contents. Federal policy may challenge the perspectives, interests, or priorities of others who, nonetheless, serve as key implementation participants. In this context, the challenge of national governance is to gain the cooperation of *reluctant partners:* implementation participants who enjoy substantial autonomy and whose cooperation is uncertain and may be difficult to achieve.

The purpose of this book is to place the problem of implementing national policy within a larger context that concerns the principles of governance in a liberal, federal polity. In that context, policy implementation is an aspect of the governing process that must balance concerns for instrumental effectiveness with constitutional principles that demand a diffuse distribution of authority.

To pursue their objectives, federal policy formulators must influence the behavior of implementation participants. However, implementation empowers its participants, placing them strategically within the policy-making process, sometimes even vesting them with resources. The ostensible purpose of implementation is instrumental: it is a means to the end for policy formulators. However, implementation also has a strategic dimension: it provides opportunities for participants to pursue self-interest. When reluctant partners implement federal policy, the process empowers potential adversaries who may discover and exploit opportunities for strategic behavior. In this sense, the implementation process becomes a paradox—the act of implementing clashes with its purpose. How can the federal government secure the cooperation it needs to implement policy when the actual act of implementing empowers potential adversaries?

DISABILITY BY DESIGN?

It can be argued that the difficulties inherent in the implementation of national policy are no accident—the U.S. government has been disabled by design. From this perspective, the stalemate that seems to occur frequently in U.S. politics is functional. If the most compelling problem of governance is to limit government, then a stalemate created by competition between authorities is desirable. Beyond competition, a diffusion of authority creates a context in which all of government is limited by the realm of its control of resources. F. A. Hayek (1960) has argued that liberalism is concerned with limiting the coercive powers of government (p. 103) and that federalism is a formula for limited government that checks the coercive power of the state: "Certain kinds of coercion require the joint and coordinated use of different powers or the employment of several means, and, if these means are in separate hands, nobody can exercise those kinds of coercion." (p. 185)

While Hayek emphasizes individual liberty and celebrates the limits of authority inherent in our system of governance, Daniel Elazar (1987) has suggested that the federal equation requires a more delicate balance: "federalism is designed to prevent tyranny without preventing governance" (p. 29). Elazar's view is that U.S. political institutions must serve contrary goals. On the one hand, governance must be conducted with respect for liberty and the legitimate diffusion of political and economic authority that exists within the United States. On the other hand, that diffusion of authority should not preclude the possibility of effective governance.

But the meaning of effective governance in a context of diffuse authority is unclear. Although constitutional principles imply that American government cannot depend upon an integrated hierarchy of authority as a means to effectiveness, many associate government with the creation and exercise of authority. Charles Lindblom (1977) has said that politics is a struggle to control authority and that "authority is as fundamental to government as exchange is to the market" (p. 13). But authority that comes from political success in a liberal democracy is limited because many resources required to accomplish positive objectives are not prizes to be won in political contests.[1] If authority is government's foundation, principles that divide authority and processes that invite or require the participation of multiple authorities would seem to be means to block public initiatives, not means to accomplish collective ends. Is governmental effectiveness—aside from effectiveness at limiting government—inconsistent with a diffuse distribution of authority?

BUILDING WITH RELUCTANT PARTNERS

The problems of implementing national policy in a liberal, federal context are illustrated by Martha Derthick's (1972) study, *New Towns In-Town*. What came to be called the "new towns" program was a brainstorm of President Lyndon Johnson, who believed that local opposition to housing the poor could be reduced if such housing were constructed on surplus federal lands. Housing built on surplus federal properties would avoid the displacement of existing residents and businesses, a common source of opposition to urban renewal initiatives. Beyond this, if land could be provided below market price, the cost of construction would be reduced, making the projects more economically feasible (p. 4).

President Johnson's vision reflected an appreciation for the politics and economics of urban renewal. Much of the controversy surrounding urban renewal initiatives in the past had come from displaced residents. As Jeffrey Henig (1985) observes, federal housing policy put government in the position of doing the "dirty work" of condemning and clearing property for redevelopment (p. 169). Often this meant that the poor were displaced in a process of gentrification or that residential units were replaced with commercial development. Avoiding this controversy was a boon for the new towns initiatives. But avoiding local political opposition was not enough—financial inducements were required to create interest among private developers. Using surplus federal land for construction sites seemed the perfect solution, reducing local political opposition while at the same time creating an attractive financial incentive for the private sector.

Despite President Johnson's apparent concern about local opposition, Derthick suggests that a major factor in the undoing of the project was the inability of federal officials to influence local government. If this was so, what was the foundation of local opposition? How did local political representatives and citizens manage to place themselves in the implementation process so well that they could constitute a powerful coalition that influenced, and ultimately overcame, an initiative of the president of the United States?

The participation of local governments in the project was a foregone conclusion. The statute authorizing federal involvement in the new towns initiative, the Housing Act of 1949, was intergovernmental: The development of programs depended upon local initiative in response to the opportunity for federal assistance. Local officials (who, for whatever reasons, are not inclined to pursue the opportunities offered by federal policy) may effectively stifle a federal initiative simply by failing to respond to the opportunity for federal assistance. If, as Derthick suggests, President Johnson wanted to use existing legislative authority to implement the new towns initiatives, it was inevitable that federalism would empower local officials as key implementors. Given this, the problem for federal officials was not to build a new town, but to induce local officials to do so.

The character of the new towns initiative suggests that federal officials were inclined to work with, rather than challenge, institutions rooted in federalism and liberalism. Former President Johnson's concerns about local opposition and economic incentives indicated tacit acceptance of the legitimacy of local political representation and respect for the integrity of the market. Thus the new towns initiatives, with these considerations, attempted to gain the cooperation of reluctant partners in pursuit of federal policy goals.

The Fort Lincoln New Town

The initial project undertaken in the new towns program was the Fort Lincoln project in Washington, D.C. It was intended as a model for the nation, and, perhaps in a perverse sense, it was. The local housing authority in the District of Columbia was authorized to receive federal grants and loans to redevelop land. The combination of presidential interest and financial incentive would seem to have been a powerful inducement for the District of Columbia to cooperate with this initiative, especially considering that the District of Columbia's local government at that time—a mayor and nine-person council—was appointed by the president himself (Derthick, 1972, p. 26). But, the wrath of President Johnson notwithstanding, local officials felt compelled to respond to citizen complaints about the Fort Lincoln proposal (pp. 27, 32).

The attention of local officials to opposition was no mere accident of local politics: it was, in part, a response to federal requirements. The participation of citizens in regional planning was a provision of federal urban renewal legislation (Henig, 1985, p. 170). Local officials were following federal guidelines by providing substantial opportunities for citizen participation and influence. Local opposition was significant and continued until the plan was modified (to be less like the president's original idea to house the poor) and the community was promised a new school.

The ambitious plan that HUD proposed in response to the president's initiative also contributed to its failure (Derthick, 1972). The plan embellished the president's proposal, calling for the development of a model community, causing local officials to doubt the feasibility of the project (p. 91). But the embellishment of the Fort Lincoln project also demonstrated the effects of federalism. The plan enhanced the importance of co-operation from local officials because extensive local services were required to make the community attractive to potential residents. HUD was asking the city for consideration in policy areas as diverse as building codes, education, and transportation. Housing policy touches many other areas of concern.

The web of intergovernmental authority that is constructed by policies that touch the jurisdiction of numerous governments complements the tendency of federalism to empower local officials. When federal officials must seek cooperation from local officials, the intentions of national policy may be frustrated if local officials fail to follow through or withhold concessions in related policy areas.

Reviewing the mixed success of several new towns initiatives, Derthick's (1972) comments reflect the ambiguous character of U.S. government. She suggests that the "failure" of the Fort Lincoln project and others is a matter of perspective.

> In shared programs, both the federal government and local governments have a political function: both play a part in defining the objectives of public action and in responding to differences in value, interest and opinion. . . . In this system, the accomplishments of government may constantly fall short of the objectives expressed at the federal level, and disillusionment follows among both the public and public officials. Such a system may nevertheless be fairly well adapted to the governing of a very large and diverse society—providing, as it does, for the expression both of abstract ideals and of particular, tangible interests. In the process of governing, the two have to be reconciled. (Pp. 101–02)

CONSTITUTIONAL PRINCIPLES AND COOPERATION

The cooperation of governments that enjoy some degree of autonomy is an implicit requirement of a federal system of governance. Elazar (1972) has said: "The idea of a federal union as a partnership is a key aspect of [U.S.] federalism." Partnership implies a diffusion of power "among several centers that must negotiate cooperative arrangements with one another in order to achieve common goals" (p. 3). Cooperation across sectors is often an implicit requirement of liberal economic organization. Lindblom (1977) has noted that constitutional rules protecting private property imply that, despite government's interest in business performance, government "cannot command business to perform"; public authority is limited to "forbid[ding] certain types of activities" and must "induce business to perform" (p. 173).[2]

Federalism

Federalism may be a source of disability for American national government. Elazar (1987) has defined federalism as "a polity of strong constituent entities and a strong general government, each possessing powers delegated to it by the people and empowered to deal directly with the citizenry in the exercise of those powers" (p. 6). He argues that federal polities are "noncentralized," meaning that the powers of government are "diffused among many centers, whose authority are guaranteed by the general constitution" (p. 34). Federal political organization must balance incompatible concerns: "Federalism is concerned simultaneously with the diffusion of political power in the name of liberty and its concentration on behalf of unity or energetic government" (p. 33).

To national policy makers federalism is a double-edged sword. Federalism provides valuable safeguards against the possible abuses of national government, protecting key political constituencies from the adverse effects of federal policy. However, federalism limits the authority of national policy makers and creates opportunities to block federal policy initiatives, regardless of their merits.

The constitutional value placed upon state and local participation is often reflected in federal legislation. Rather than seeking to minimize federalism, federal policy initiatives are likely to reflect its values by requiring that policy is implemented in conjunction with institutions of state and local government. Elazar (1972) notes that the Congress has been inclined to provide a substantial role for state governments, even in those areas where exclusive federal jurisdiction seems well established in the Constitution (p. 50). The tendency to reflect and reaffirm the value of shared authority in federal statutes provides opportunities for states and localities to participate in the implementation of federal policy. Participation implies representation of interest and, if state or local interests are not compatible with federal program goals, states and localities may use their autonomy to develop and pursue strategic responses to the federal initiative, undermining or circumventing the intentions of federal policy.

Complexity—the interdependence of policy issues and decisions—multiplies the influence of state and local governments in federal decisions. This is clear from the Fort Lincoln example since HUD sought numerous concessions from the District of Columbia government for its ambitious plan. But even when federal policy initiatives are carefully crafted to minimize the role of states and localities, they are likely to touch upon the jurisdiction of numerous organizations within various governments. No policy domain is immune. The production of nuclear munitions has been threatened by state actions to block nuclear waste deposits within their territory. The state's interest in protecting the health and well-being of its residents has become a basis for influencing federal decisions on weapons production. Officials in Nevada delayed federal site studies of the proposed Yucca Mountain nuclear waste repository by refusing to issue necessary permits (*Washington Post,* 10/3/89, p. A1). Subsequently, a Nevada law prohibiting the storage of high-level nuclear waste within the state was held nonbinding on the federal government by the U.S. Circuit Court of Appeals, clearing the way for continued site inspections on Yucca Mountain (*Washington Post,* 9/20/90, p. A17).

Liberalism

Liberalism is another possible source of disability for U.S. national government. In a market economy, entrepreneurs exercise authority and control resources important to social well-being. While this form of economic organization is valued by policy formulators, it also provides opportunities for strategic behavior that can twist and distort the intentions of federal policy and undermine the achievement of federal goals.

The desire for market efficiency and innovation is one motive for liberal economic organization.[3] However, a more cynical interpretation of the political value of liberalism is that business firms are attractive targets for policy initiatives that serve to resolve politically sensitive questions. Policy that targets business can be a politically expedient way to increase costs to voters. Political leaders can credibly argue that business regulation is carried out in the public interest; increased costs to consumers are hidden, indirect, and imposed by business, not political, leadership.

In the United States private property rights are important constitutional and political values. However, private property rights limit public authority and establish the commercial sector as a legitimate rival to government. The ability of government to control business for the public good is constrained by our strong desire to protect the integrity of business.

By placing control of so many important resources in private hands, liberal economic organization implies that federal policy formulators are often compelled to seek cooperation from business to pursue national policy goals. Any sort of government intervention into the market is bound to be controversial, as popular objections to "federal intrusion" into the marketplace would suggest. However, Hayek (1960) has argued that economic policy is a legitimate activity for government as long as the state confines its power of coercion to a "legal framework" (p. 222). Beyond this, government may engage in any economic activity; however, it cannot use its coercive powers (p. 223). Hayek's interpretation of liberal philosophy is open to government intervention into the market as long as it does not unduly interfere with the "private sphere" (p. 139).

> Freedom of economic activity had meant freedom under the law, not the absence of all government action. The "interference" or "intervention" of government which those writers [Adam Smith or John Stuart Mill] opposed as a matter of principle therefore meant only the infringement of the private sphere which the general rules of law were intended to protect. They did not mean that government should never concern itself with any economic matters. But they did mean that there were certain kinds of governmental measures that should be precluded on principle and which could not be justified on any grounds of expediency. (Pp. 220–21)

Though Hayek would likely agree with critics of federal intervention into the market who argue that it is ill-advised and often ineffective—as exemplified by the Fort Lincoln project—his agreement would be based upon arguments about expediency, not upon claims that liberal constitutional values preclude "federal intrusion." While Hayek's (1960) interpretation of liberalism does not preclude federal intervention into the market, it does establish two broad categories of intervention that are consistent with liberal principles. The first is intervention that is rooted in a legal framework or in "general rules specifying conditions which everybody engaging in a certain activity must satisfy" (p. 224). The second is intervention in which government does not use coercive power and instead induces voluntary cooperation through the use of incentives. Federal intervention in the Fort Lincoln project would seem to be an example of the second type.

Contradictory Demands

Pogo once said: "We have met the enemy and he is us!" Our principles of governance imply a similar contradiction—it can be disputed whether the disability of government is cause for concern or for celebration. By demanding that government be constituted on principles that divide authority in order to protect individual liberty, have we created a government that can do nothing else? Must concern for liberty be sacrificed to improve the capacity of government to accomplish its policy objectives? Can U.S. government be, at once, limited and effective?

When governments share jurisdiction and when authority to make key social decisions is further divided between government and the commercial sector, national governance requires cooperation. Alternatives to cooperation form a short, unpromising list.[4] If cooperation cannot be induced by command, the limits of national leadership are often defined by the inclination of reluctant partners to cooperate and the difficulties of implementation may be understood as problems of inducing cooperation within a context of diffuse authority.

Though it is unclear whether this disability of government should be regarded as a problem, the implication of principles that demand diffuse authority is clear: Implementation participants are often free to respond strategically—in a calculated, self-interested manner—to the demands of federal policy. Some failures of federal policy may be manifestations of this difficulty. Federal authority, limited by constitutional principles, invites strategic behavior, making it difficult to translate the authority to control some limited, oblique tools of public policy into the ability of the federal government to accomplish its ends.

If so, the limits of federal power are real, creating the dilemma that federal policy makers so often confront: How can the federal government hope to accomplish national policy goals when potential adversaries must be embraced as partners during the implementation process? If the ability to govern is rooted in authority, adherence to constitutional principles cannot but diminish the ability of the federal government to achieve its ends.

DISABILITY AND PARADOX

It can be argued that the implementation process is a paradox if reluctant partners dilute the authority of federal officials and, thereby, diminish the ability of national government to achieve its ends. When reluctant partners are brought into the implementation process, their participation and natural inclination for representation of interest may limit available options or redirect public resources to the service of their particular agenda. The Fort Lincoln project suggests that the ability of the national government to induce cooperation—even in highly favorable circumstances—is limited and depends upon the uncertain and undependable inclinations of implementation participants.

Constitutional principles that make it difficult for national government to accomplish its policy objectives also have another important effect—they make it relatively easy for well-positioned interests to enjoy protection from harm. If so, it may be that U.S. politics is truly "defensive"—serving the primary purpose of protecting a few well-positioned interests from harm by frustrating the general will as expressed through national policy decisions.

A Dissenting View

It is plausible to interpret the Fort Lincoln project as evidence of the disability of government. Certainly, it is an example in which some federal leaders failed to achieve their ends when dealing with reluctant partners. However, before accepting the conclusion that the efficacy of the U.S. government is doomed by its own constitutional principles, let us delve a bit more into its source. At the foundation of this view is a conception of governance that is rooted in authority. If government is equated with authority, the power to govern is found in the ability to issue commands. A diffuse distribution of authority implies that government must be limited either to narrowly drawn purposes within the scope of its formal control or to pursuit of those objectives in common to all who share authority. Thus, the central concern of politics is who controls authority.

Clarence Stone (1989) has offered an alternative view based upon a distinction between two types of political power—"power over" as distinct from "power to." According to Stone, power struggles concern "not control and resistance, but gaining and fusing a capacity to act" (p. 229). From this perspective, political power is the "power to" accomplish things. If society is not neatly integrated into a hierarchy of command and control, the problem of governance cannot be reduced to the question of who holds authority over others. Instead—assuming that numerous centers of authority exist, each pursuing its own ends— the purpose of governance is not to command, but to create the capacity to act—to create the "power to" accomplish collective goals. This is done by creating arrangements that allow numerous authorities to cooperate to achieve collective goals. From Stone's perspective, the central concern of politics is how this capacity to act is realized and what effect its realization has upon its potential to act and the evolution of policy over time.

For the implementation process, the difference is fundamental. From the "power over" perspective, the power of the government is zero sum. Consequently, the ability to govern is diminished by additional implementation participants, especially if they are reluctant partners.[5] From the "power to" perspective, power is positive sum—the participation of other authorities *creates* power; not only are implementation participants empowered, the federal government itself is empowered when national policy creates terms for cooperation and coordination of policy among numerous centers of authority.

This revised conception of power implies that implementation is the generation of the capacity to undertake programs to accomplish national policy goals. Given a diffusion of authority to control key resources, the implementation process must establish conditions that facilitate cooperation among social institutions or organizations that control resources key to policy success, and join their resources, perhaps even orchestrate their activities, to create a coherent capacity to act without unifying control.

LEADERSHIP AND DIFFUSE AUTHORITY

This book is based upon the view that the implementation process concerns the "power to" accomplish collective goals. From this perspective, the essential task of the implementation process is to create a context in which participants are likely to cooperate to achieve national policy goals despite the absence of a dominating authority. In this most fundamental sense, implementation is a political problem: It is a manifestation of tension built into the most basic political structures of liberal democracy—tension between a diffusion of authority to protect liberty and a concentration of authority to promote effective government.

In this context, one cannot assume that cooperation among implementation participants follows automatically from their mutual interests, so the implementation process must be examined to determine whether context or mechanisms exist that enhance the incentives for cooperation. Emphasis upon cooperation is unusual in the implementation literature. Top-down approaches value compliance over cooperation. Bottom-up approaches focus upon conflict resolution but fail to ask how implementation participants might realize their mutual interest through cooperation.

Given a system of governance that widely distributes authority and the continuing prospect of an active national policy agenda, the problems of organizing and maintaining cooperation during the implementation process are a key focus for investigation. Why are some conflicts of interest resolved cooperatively while others end in policy stagnation? How can policy formulators or implementors create a context in which constructive patterns of cooperation are likely to emerge? What aspects of policy design promote or retard the possibilities for cooperation during the implementation process?

These questions guide this inquiry. The main points of my argument may be sketched as follows. Principles of political and economic organization in the United States make the federal government depend on the cooperation of other authorities to achieve its policy goals. Most existing approaches to implementation analysis view the ability of government to gain compliance with commands as the key to implementation effectiveness. Despite generating important insights into the implementation paradox, existing approaches downplay the importance of cooperation and seek either to consolidate federal authority or to abandon federal leadership. The *implementation regime framework* can infuse constitutional principles that undergird the political economy of the United States into the implementation literature. Developed from the literature on cooperation and international regime development, the regime framework identifies contextual conditions, organizational strategies, and policy actions that can help to gain the cooperation of reluctant partners.

CONCLUSION

Richard Nelson (1977) has said: "The key role of analysis is to place the problem in an appropriate context so that one can begin to describe the nature of possible solutions" (p. 148). In this book, I place the implementation problem in the context of diffuse authority demanded by the principles of political and economic organization in the United States. A diffuse distribution of authority complicates the development and implementation of national policy and implies that cooperation among numerous centers of authority is often the key to effectiveness.

In the following chapters, the problems of and potential for cooperation in the implementation of national policy in the United States are explored through the presentation and illustration of the implementation regime framework. In chapter 2 I identify and take issue with the most common themes of the implementation literature and examine ways in which the problem of arranging cooperation during the implementation process has been treated. In chapter 3, the implementation regime framework—a framework that seeks to reconcile the strategic and instrumental roles of implementation participants—is presented and elaborated. Chapter 4 discusses ideal regime types and the normative propositions that underlie them. The possibility of policy reform and the process of regime development is illustrated in chapter 5 with the presentation of a case study of the National School Lunch Program. In chapter 6, the difficult problem of implementing policy that imposes costs is discussed through consideration of the ongoing controversy about where to locate a nuclear waste repository. Chapter 7 presents a summary, implications, and conclusions.

2 AUTHORITY, EXCHANGE, AND GOVERNANCE

HOW HAVE the problems of cooperation and policy coordination been cast in the implementation literature? At the risk of overlooking some differences in emphasis, this chapter identifies and discusses two perspectives on the implementation problem. Most often, the implementation process has been viewed as a problem of organization—the essence of effective implementation is to design an instrument to achieve objectives identified by federal policy formulators. This conception of the problem equates governmental effectiveness with federal authority and control of the implementation process and implies that cooperation is induced by command. The alternative view within the literature sees implementation as an exchange relationship. From this perspective, implementation is an order—an institution that provides a context for interaction but which lacks the goal orientation of organization. This view of the problem equates the effectiveness of implementation with compromise and accommodation and implies that cooperation is induced through bargaining.

To review theory in the implementation literature one must confront the difficulty of bringing coherence to a field that has tended toward case analyses and situational explanations of implementation outcomes. To overcome this difficulty, two social relationships described by Charles Lindblom (1977)—authority and exchange—anchor this review. Lindblom argues that authority and exchange underlie two types of social organization—bureaucracies and markets. Often treated in the implementation literature as ideals, these models of social organization frame issues and propose solutions to the problems of inducing cooperation during the implementation process.

Lindblom defines authority as the designation of a person or body, by coercion or voluntary consent, to make binding decisions for others (1977, pp. 17–18). From this perspective, implementation is a problem of organization in the sense described by Philip Selznick: "organization . . . is a technical instrument for mobilizing human energies and directing them toward set aims . . . an expendable tool, a rational instrument engineered to do a job" (1957, p. 5). F. A. Hayek describes the difference between an organization, rooted in authority, and a spontaneous order, based upon exchange:

> In contrast to an organization, neither has a spontaneous order a purpose nor need there be agreement on the concrete results it will produce in order to agree on the desirability of such an order, because, being independent of any particular purpose, it can be used for, and will assist in the pursuit of, a great many different, divergent and even conflicting individual purposes. Thus the order of the market, in particular, rests not on common purposes but on reciprocity, that is on the reconciliation of different purposes for the mutual benefit of the participants. (1967, p. 163).

In the context of an order, cooperation is induced by exchanging something of value for it. Lindblom defines exchange as the acceptance of contingent offers of mutually beneficial reward (1977, pp. 33–34). From this perspective, the implementation process is concerned primarily with the satisfaction of implementation participants. The process lacks direction or purpose aside from reconciliation of conflict between the participants.

Organization is an instrument designed to achieve an identified purpose. The purposes of national policy are found in the intentions of federal policy formulators. In contrast, an order, such as a market system, structures the interaction of many individuals who may have conflicting purposes, allowing them to reconcile their differences through exchange. The difference between these perspectives is important to implementation theory: viewing the implementation process as an organization, one emphasizes the instrumental role of implementation participants and seeks to resolve the implementation paradox by deeming strategic behavior to be illegitimate during the implementation process. In viewing the implementation process as an order, one emphasizes the strategic role of implementors—interaction is seen as an end in itself—and whatever result is produced by the clash of interest is accepted as the proper outcome.[1]

THE ORGANIZATION OF AUTHORITY

From the perspective of the authority paradigm, wisdom and legitimacy reside in the federal government; the task of implementation analysis is to establish "the extent to which legally-mandated objectives were achieved over time and why" (Sabatier, 1986, p. 22). Implementation here is viewed as a problem of efficient production because the purpose of the process is taken as given: "value laden" decisions about policy goals are assumed to be beyond legitimate dispute. When purpose is given, the implementation problem is reduced to efficiency and control: what is the best way to manipulate implementors to achieve established ends? The authority paradigm seeks a rational connection of means and ends and thus tends toward the rational hierarchy exemplified by bureaucracy as its preferred organizational instrument.

If bureaucratic order is the ideal model of social organization, social relationships are well-organized when conditions are created to support bureaucratic control: Authority is rule-governed and arranged hierarchically; clear communication from policy formulators down to subordinates is established; performance of subordinates is monitored and evaluated; deviant behavior, when detected, is sanctioned by higher authority in accord with established rules. Social organization is problematic if conditions required for bureaucratic order are violated; ambiguous directives, fragmented or inadequate authority, and overlapping jurisdiction are common examples of such conditions.

In authority relationships, cooperation is equated with compliance. Amitai Etzioni has observed that "there are two parties to a compliance relationship: an actor who exercises power, and an actor, subject to this power, who responds to this subjection" (1975, p. 4). The purpose of cooperation is to coordinate the activities of those subject to authority in order to make their behavior correspond to the desires of those who exercise authority. Etzioni (p. 5) identifies three forms of power that may be applied to establish compliance within an organization: coercive power, remunerative power, and normative power. Coercive power is "the application, or the threat of application, of physical sanctions . . . or controlling through force the satisfaction of needs." Remunerative power is "based upon control of material resources and rewards." Normative power is found in the "allocation and manipulation of symbolic rewards and deprivations."

Carrots and Sticks

The portion of the implementation literature that is grounded in the authority paradigm often focuses upon the use of coercive and remunerative power. A common expression used to describe the means available to the federal government for inducing cooperation from others is "the carrot and the stick." This implies that federal policy is designed to influence the behavior of implementors with a combination of reward and punish-

ment—arrangements that offer incentives or enforce discipline
consistent with federal objectives.

The expression calls to mind a horse driven by a coachman.
Whether the horse is chasing the carrot or running from the
stick, he is an instrument manipulated according to the driver's
will. The use of punishment or reward is a matter of expediency—or possibly kindness—but not a consequence of viewing the horse as a partner whose political status commands
respect and accommodation. The coachman's authority is absolute; his power is checked only by the instruments available
to him and his interest in effectively directing the horse. Treatment that is too harsh or too stingy may make the horse difficult
to handle, frustrating the coachman's intentions. But it is expediency, not principle, that guides the coachman as he drives
the horse.

To many, the coachman is an apt metaphor for the federal
government. This is a seductive vision. The unity of command
given life by the coachman suggests coherence in public purpose. If the coachman knows the horse, the animal can be
readily marshalled and directed toward his ends: a vision of
competent government with coherence of purpose.

If the norms and proper procedures of public decision making are observed, the power of government to induce cooperation lies in authority—legitimate power. The coercive authority
of government—its ability to enforce discipline through punishment—flows from the stick. But, though the carrot is an
incentive, it is no less a manifestation of authority than the
stick, for it is offered as a condition of compliance. This is
remunerative power. Dangled just beyond reach, the carrot
tempts the horse to motion; unwittingly, he exerts himself for
the coachman's ends. Though remunerative power is less likely
to alienate the subject (Etzioni, 1975), it remains a means employed to gain compliance. But this is as it should be—the relationship of the coachman to the horse is that of master to beast
of burden.

If effective governance is equated with control of resources
and the ability to marshal them to pursue an established goal,

the all-powerful coachman is indeed an attractive vision. Perhaps this is why so much of the implementation literature reflects this view; implicitly, the power to accomplish national policy objectives is equated with the extent to which federal policy formulators or their agents in bureaucracy control the implementation process. A problem which analysts often consider is the design of instruments of control. How can one be sure that the stick conveys "the right message"? Might an apple be more enticing to implementors than a carrot? In spite of differences in method, emphasis, or approach, the implementation literature grounded in the authority paradigm is based upon a common premise: effective implementation is rooted in authority and control; whatever diminishes control of the process by federal authorities is the enemy of effectiveness.

Analyzing the problems of implementing national policy in this manner tends to focus on identifying conditions that undermine federal authority. Three conditions that might diminish prospects for implementation success are: (1) the limits of federal authority resulting from constitutional principles—federalism and liberalism; (2) the limits of rationality in policy design—the impossibility of knowing in advance what implications of federal authority can be established; and (3) the tendency of implementation participants to exploit the implementation process by behaving strategically (Bardach, 1980). Proposals in response to the implementation problem often treat constitutional principles as obstacles to be overcome, seeking to consolidate federal authority or to limit the damage done by strategic behavior during the implementation process.[2]

The authority paradigm treats implementors as mere instruments—tools to be manipulated at the will of the federal government. The preceding chapter suggested, however, that implementation participants are often important political entities in their own right. If so, it may be inappropriate to think of the implementation process in a liberal, federal polity as being "effective" to the extent that it is controlled by "the carrot and the stick." The expression betrays a lack of appreciation for the political standing of implementation participants.

AUTHORITY IN IMPLEMENTATION THEORY

From the perspective of the authority paradigm, implementation is a production process whose purpose is to generate policy
outputs consistent with the intentions of federal policy formulators. The implementation process begins at the top and
proceeds down through a hierarchy of organizations; the decision output from each organization becomes an input to the
following one. The federal policy initiative is the catalyst that
causes the federal program sponsor to develop program details
and requirements. These federal requirements become an input
to other implementation participants, who then create state or
local programs in response. Although the federal policy initiative sparks the process, problems of bureaucratic control and
diffuse authority make it difficult for federal policy formulators
to control the process and direct it toward their desired end.
This is the essence of the "implementation problem."

Implementation problems have many sources, but they
often begin with the distortion or miscommunication of the intentions of federal policy formulators. On the federal level, bureaucratic insubordination or lethargy may divert or derail a
federal initiative (Montjoy and O'Toole, 1979; Edwards, 1980;
Baum, 1984). On the intergovernmental level, federalism may
result in slippage or mutation of federal intentions (Derthick,
1972; Van Horn and Van Meter, 1976; Elmore, 1978; Berman,
1978; O'Toole and Montjoy, 1984). The issue is whether the
program as implemented is consistent with the objectives of federal policy formulators, or if it is merely symbolic or not adopted
at all.

Sequential Decision Making

The authority paradigm views the implementation process
as a sequence of decisions that may move the process toward
or away from the federal policy objective. James Thompson
(1967) has described a model of sequential interdependence
that reveals important aspects of this conception of the implementation process. He argues that sequential interdependence

is not symmetric—the importance of a link, rather, is related to its position in the process. The earlier in the sequence that a linkage occurs, the more critical it is. This is especially true with an organizational process in which a single central unit serves several parallel processes (e.g., a federal governing arrangement in which the national policy spawns numerous parallel state or local policies).

Thompson's analysis implies that federal agencies are the most important implementation participants and, therefore, the most pressing implementation problem is to gain control of federal executive agencies.[3] This creates concern about whether the means available to policy formulators for controlling bureaucratic organizations is strong enough. Control is the key issue. How can federal policy formulators hope to control the implementation process if their own house is not in order? Federal program sponsors—lead agencies charged with the authority to implement federal policy—are more likely to be effective advocates for the federal position if they are effectively controlled. Failure to control federal program sponsors is a mistake that is likely to be compounded as federal policy objectives are misrepresented or disregarded later in the implementation process.

The importance of federal agencies in the implementation process is independent of the magnitude of the effect they may have upon the behavior of other implementation participants or the final contents of policy (a counterpoint to those who would argue that "street level" personnel are most important). Thompson's analysis implies that even if the influence of the federal program sponsor is slight, the existence of numerous parallel processes within the system multiplies the importance of its influence many times. To control the implementation process, federal policy makers must first gain control of their agents in the federal bureaucracy.

COOPERATION AND IMPLEMENTATION FAILURE

Thompson's view of sequential decision making conveys a clear message about the implementation process: its performance is fragile. When decisions are made in sequence, the chain of organizations that forms the implementation process is only as strong as its weakest link. Failure at any point in the sequence is sufficient enough to cause the whole system to fail.

Within the implementation process, participants may decide to cooperate with the proposal that has been passed down from the preceding implementation participant or to resist it. Federal policy formulators must convince implementation participants to commit their efforts to the pursuit of federal policy goals. The decision to cooperate or resist is thought to depend upon the extent to which implementation participants are in conflict with the policy objective.[4] Of course, federal policy formulators may attempt to manipulate the inclinations of implementors by using rewards or sanctions.

Interorganizational complexity and conflict are complementary explanations for implementation failure. Complexity in the implementation process—usually indicated by the number of links in a path of decisions required for implementation to be completed—reduces the probability of implementation success if the probability of success at each link is less than one. Implementation failure is an inevitable result of the fragile nature of a system that distributes a veto to so many participants. The existence of numerous veto points is often taken as evidence of undue complexity, a circumstance in which the number of implementation participants could be reduced while still maintaining the quality of the product. Conflict—a low probability of cooperation at any point in the sequence—diminishes the probability of implementation success because individual participants are more likely to resist. A combination of complexity and conflict is a sure formula for failure. With the process so fragile, one should be pleasantly surprised if implementation does not go awry.

Strategic Behavior in the Implementation Process

The authority paradigm recognizes that diffuse authority may create opportunities for strategic behavior. However, rather than seeing diffuse authority as a reflection of constitutional values, or even as a constraint within which existing institutions must operate, diffuse authority is viewed as a problem to be solved.

If participants behave strategically, seeking opportunities to exploit the process, implementation may be viewed as a game. Eugene Bardach (1980), who views implementation as an "assembly" process—in which the elements required to produce desired policy outcomes must be brought together within a context in which implementors are opportunistic—works within the authority paradigm because he assumes that the proper course of policy has been set prior to the implementation process. In other words, a neat separation of means and ends has been imposed upon the policy-making process. Given this, implementation is an organizational problem: How can one accomplish the established ends?

Difficulties arise during implementation if participants behave strategically. Participants are seen as players in a game who make choices based upon their self-interested evaluation of the likely consequences of their actions. Bardach contends that discretion in the implementation process can undermine implementation performance, that strategic behavior can drive up costs or twist federal intentions, causing the initiative to jump off track. To avoid the disruptions that implementation games can bring, he proposes a "fixer" to monitor implementation behavior and propose changes in policy that may be required.

Implicit in Bardach's analysis is the view that strategic behavior during the implementation process is politically illegitimate (and thus should be repressed). Rather than viewing strategic behavior as an indication of legitimate political conflict, it is seen as a cost the federal government is compelled to pay by participants who exploit their position in the implementation process.

Evaluating Implementation Performance

Overhead democracy, a conception of the policy-making process that narrowly defines and strictly separates implementation from policy formulation, is the normative foundation of the authority paradigm.[5] This is a strong, if not wholly appropriate, foundation from which to evaluate implementation performance in a liberal, federal polity. From this perspective, legitimate policy making requires that the policy's objectives be expressed by elected representatives through the institutional mechanisms of the policy formulation process. Implementation is limited to the faithful and efficient translation of policy objectives into action; the production of the policy product envisioned by policy formulators. Deviation from policy formulators' vision is considered to be dysfunctional behavior that results from illegitimate political motives; illegitimate because it is assumed that any legitimate social conflict relevant to implementation activities has been resolved during policy formulation.

To avoid the possibility of illegitimate political influence, policy formulators may attempt to "program" implementation by specifying in detail, and in every conceivable contingency, the desired implementation behavior (Berman, 1980; Sharp, 1981). Of course, the problem of programming implementation participants can be minimized by selecting implementing organizations that are committed to the policy objective (Mazmanian and Sabatier, 1983) or by carefully manipulating the incentives of implementation participants (Mitnick and Backoff, 1984). Those who apply the authority paradigm but lack faith in comprehensive policy design (e.g., Bardach) will instead closely monitor the process and intervene to "fix" problems as they occur.

The distinction drawn between the role of policy formulators and implementors implies a standard by which implementation performance may be judged: policy formulators identify policy objectives and select policy alternatives; implementors take action, directed by policy choice. The appropriate standards by which implementation performance is judged are efficiency and fidelity. Whatever stands between policy choice and the realization of policy formulators' plans inhibits their ability to govern. The point of policy design, then, is to anticipate gaps or leaks in federal authority and to propose the means to correct them.

The prevailing view of the implementation process and its role in American governance is now clear: from the perspective of the authority paradigm, the implementation process is an instrument, a means to the ends of higher authority. Consequently, implementation is viewed as an organizational problem: the implementation process should be designed to accomplish the purposes defined at earlier stages of the policy-making process. Whether chasing the carrot or running from the stick, implementors are subordinates manipulated by rewards or punishment meted out by the coachman.

AUTHORITY AND THE IMPLEMENTATION PARADOX

Implementation is a paradox because it is difficult to accomplish national policy objectives when the act of implementing empowers potential adversaries. With its emphasis on control, the authority paradigm is consistent with this view. Diffuse authority, especially authority in the hands of adversaries, is a formula for failure. To resolve the implementation paradox, ways must be found to enhance the control over the implementation process that national policy formulators enjoy.

The authority paradigm proposes three strategies to avoid the implementation paradox. One is to bypass implementation practices that share public authority by expanding the exclusive authority of the federal government, creating hierarchical lines of authority where none had existed previously. Under this sort of proposal, agents of the federal government would directly administer federal policy on a national scale, bypassing reluctant partners and the problems they create. Obviously, this suggestion conflicts with constitutional principles that value diffuse authority. Beyond this, it may be impossible to create a realm of exclusive policy authority for the federal government, even with a limited federal agenda.

Alternatively, federal policy formulators could seek to consolidate their authority within the federal system by requiring reluctant partners to cooperate by mandating participation, developing performance criteria, and administering sanctions for noncompliance. This proposal is at odds with constitutional principles that value diffuse authority, and it also can be questioned on grounds of feasibility. In a world of dynamic problems and diffuse authority, consolidation of federal authority within the intergovernmental system may not be possible, even if it were desirable. Anthony Downs (1967) has noted that "delegation . . . accompanied by variances in officials' goals" creates a "leakage of authority" (p. 134). Since delegation of authority is a requirement in any sort of organization, one must assume that authorities at the top are never completely able to control the behavior of those at the bottom. Charles Lindblom has observed that the impossibility of absolute control of authority implies that unintended consequences are likely: "Because there is no complex organization in which authority can be constrained within limits intended by those who establish it, authority always becomes to a degree uncontrollable. Grant an official authority to do a job, and he will also use it to do other things not intended for him" (1977, p. 24).

Given the difficulties inherent in the creation of exclusive federal authority or the consolidation of federal authority, it is always possible to argue for limited government. Accepting the view that the U.S. government is disabled by design, the impossibility of solving problems through the development of comprehensive authority can be read as an argument in favor of limiting the public agenda: Let government do only those few things that are within its competence to control.

CRITICISMS OF THE AUTHORITY PARADIGM

The authority paradigm overlooks the important distinction between subordinates—federal agencies that serve as federal program sponsors—and political rivals—intermediaries who enjoy a legitimate base of political support outside federal policy-making processes and who may be reluctant partners. A more accurate view of the policy-making process would distinguish different sorts of implementation participants to avoid the normative ambiguity and confusion that comes from applying the same standards of compliance to both.

Much of the analysis done under the authority paradigm implicitly assumes that policy formulators and their institutions are capable of synoptic policy planning. This implies that policy formulators are able to anticipate what aspects of policy would be sources of ambiguity or difficulty during implementation and, further, to create and convey terms, through written directives, on which these matters are to be settled.[6] Unless this assumption is made, the notion of compliance with directives becomes ambiguous. If the problem is to gain compliance, what does compliance mean in an imperfect world? Is compliance following rules and directives to the letter? If so, synoptic planning is required to avoid the execution of flawed policy. Does compliant behavior include a license to correct policy that seems to require adjustment to local circumstances or to unforeseen contingencies? If so, how can adjustments made under the reasonable license to correct flaws be distinguished from obstruction or cunning behavior?

The standards by which the authority paradigm evaluates implementation performance imply that all legitimate conflict has been resolved prior to the initiation of the implementation process. However, it may not be possible for policy formulators to comprehensively resolve conflict. If it is impossible to identify in advance those matters that create conflict during implementation (due to the cognitive limits of policy formulators or due to the variety of circumstances and the dynamic nature of policy problems), some degree of proposal modification could be regarded as functional, or even necessary, for implementation. If legitimate conflict exists, conflict resolution and political representation may become important aspects of the implementation process (Rein and Rabinovitz, 1978).

The limited rationality of policy formulators or their institutional processes and a need for conflict resolution implies a final criticism which greatly expands the scope of implementation activities. If unanticipated problems may emerge, or if legitimate conflict remains to be resolved, policy may continue to be developed as it is implemented. An evolutionary view of policy making emerges in which initiatives evolve toward a workable solution through the activities of the implementation process (see Majone and Wildavsky, 1983). Effective implementation would require that imprecise policies be fleshed-out or that defective policies be corrected, as they are implemented, through adjustments to local conditions or unforeseen contingencies. Policy evolution is incompatible with the authority paradigm and its emphasis upon control, implying instead an "adaptive" conception of implementation (Berman, 1980; Sharp, 1981).

Taking policy goals as given, the authority paradigm seeks effective means to accomplish established ends. This confuses the problems of bureaucratic control with the problems of intergovernmental and cross-sectoral cooperation, implying inappropriate standards for evaluating implementation performance. The authority paradigm, placing faith in the rationality of federal policy formulators and their ability to resolve social conflict, proposes solutions to implementation problems that are inconsistent with key constitutional principles. An objection to this view, and to the analysis that applies it, is that it confuses problems of organization with problems of governance.

EXCHANGE AND THE MARKET MODEL

From the perspective of the exchange paradigm, the purposes of federal policy are often ambiguous or contradictory and federal domination of the implementation process is a myth. Implementation studies often conclude that the reality of the implementation process is in its diffuse distribution of authority—no one is in charge—where conflict resolution and bargaining are important determinants of the course of policy.

Since circumstances and context vary from case to case, knowledge is particular and situational, and effective problem solving requires a diffuse distribution of authority which allows key participants to adjust policy to the task at hand. Policy evolution is inevitable and constructive. The purpose of analysis is to understand the problems, perspectives, and interaction of implementation participants at the contact point between public programs and citizens (Weikart and Banet, 1976; McLaughlin, 1976; Berman, 1978; Elmore, 1982).

From this perspective, incentives and self-interest play a crucial role in implementation. Implementation participants are assumed to be of equal status, but may differ in their ability to influence each other. Cooperation and policy coordination occur through exchange. The purpose of exchange is the mutual benefit of the participants, so the values relevant to policy decisions are those brought to the process and expressed as preferences by participants. As exchange relationships are based upon cooperation resulting from the pursuit of self-interest, the scope of cooperation (and, by implication, federal policy) is constrained by the interests of implementation participants. Exchange will not take place if it is not beneficial to all; Lindblom notes that this is an extreme form of mutual adjustment (1977, p. 32).

EXCHANGE IN IMPLEMENTATION THEORY

Viewed from the exchange perspective, implementation is a relationship in which each participant contributes something of value. The key to exchange is reciprocity. Typically, the federal government provides resources (financial and authoritative) to intermediaries who cooperate in pursuit of federal policy objectives.

The concrete nature of implementation activities compels implementors to reconsider and resolve the costs and contradictions of the initiative that were repressed or unknown during policy formulation (Stone, 1980). Consequently, policy initiatives evolve as they move through the implementation process and respond to changes in practice, perspective, and value that such movement suggests. Herein lies a potential problem. Policy evolution is constructive because it introduces flexibility and local rationality into the development of policy. But, lacking clear standards to monitor policy evolution, it is difficult to distinguish constructive changes or adjustments to local circumstances from goal displacement. This difficulty is compounded when policy evolves in an environment characterized by "low visibility" (Stone, 1980).

Successful implementation requires accommodation among implementation participants. Otherwise, the initiative is transformed, derailed, or undermined during the implementation process. This is a clean break with the authority paradigm. Rather than viewing implementation as a means to achieving the policy formulators' ends, implementation is seen as a legitimate source of political power for its participants. When viewed as an exchange relationship, the fundamental dynamic of the implementation process is the adaptation of the program to its local organizational context (Berman, 1978).

This implies that prudent policy formulators must consider and accommodate the interests of implementation participants during policy design. If this is done, the implementation process becomes a constraint upon policy choice, and policy is bent toward the interests and perspectives of implementation participants. Acceptable policy is likely to be incremental, reducing federal leadership to the anemic purpose of marginal change to existing organizational values.

The exchange paradigm is pessimistic about the potential for effective policy, suggesting that the real beneficiaries of government policy are often those that implement it, not the supposed clients.[7] Beyond this, policy that is transformed by implementation participants has little instrumental value unless the implementors' self-interest can be harnessed to create socially desirable outcomes. For these reasons, those who view public bureaucracy as a problem often feature the exchange paradigm in analysis that supports the replacement of administered policy with pseudomarkets.

Cooperation and Exchange

When implementation is an exchange relationship, the process is a bargaining game in which well-positioned interests compete for control of the program or other prized resources. From this perspective, policy outputs are created by the interaction of key actors from organizations in the implementation process (Edner, 1976), not passed sequentially from one level down to the next. The outcome of the interaction is beyond the control of any single participant and results from the intersection of the participants' choices (Allison, 1971; Elmore, 1978). The outcome may be unintended and should not be taken to indicate the wishes of federal policy formulators or the intentions of implementation participants.

Reciprocal Decision Making

The exchange paradigm is based upon a specific model of decision making which assumes that interdependence within the implementation process is reciprocal (Thompson, 1967). This type of interdependence requires at least two autonomous participants, each of whose behavior effects the other. The outcome from the interaction is determined by the intersection of their choices. In this context, bargaining may be explicit or tacit and can occur even when one player "moves first," if other participants can later veto the initiative.

In figure 1 an example of reciprocal decision making is presented. Two participants are identified, the federal program sponsor and a local intermediary. Each participant may select one of two possible strategies, cooperation or defection. Cooperation is the willingness to adapt the program to address other implementation participants' concerns. Defection is the unwillingness to compromise during implementation, the in-

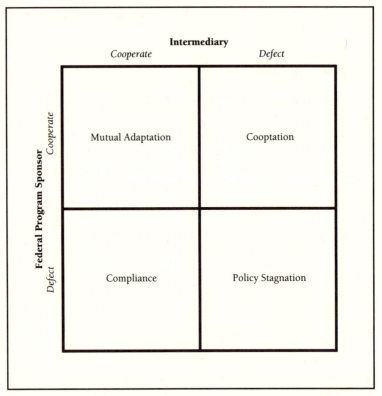

FIG. 1.   Reciprocal Decision Making in the Implementation Process

sistence on operating the program in terms most favorable to one's interest. The intersection of these strategies creates four possible outcomes.

When both participants cooperate, implementation occurs through "mutual adaptation" as policy evolves toward a workable compromise that reflects the concerns of the implementation participants (see McLaughlin, 1976; Berman, 1978). When the intermediary alone defects, cooptation occurs; federal policy is modified to accommodate the interests of the intermediary. When the federal sponsor alone defects, compliance is gained from the intermediary as the federal program is implemented on the terms demanded by the sponsor without sub-stantial modification. When both participants defect, policy stagnation occurs. This list of outcomes is exhaustive for two players with two strategic options.

A similar scheme was applied by Milbrey McLaughlin in her report on implementing education innovation (1976). McLaughlin found outcomes within only three of the four categories. The empty category was that in which the federal sponsor gains compliance from the intermediary. This suggests that it may be difficult for federal program sponsors to impose programs upon other implementation participants and, further, that the result of such efforts is often policy stagnation. But perhaps the most important aspect of McLaughlin's analysis is the positive claims she makes for mutual adaptation.

> Where implementation was successful, and where significant change in participant attitudes, skills, and behavior occurred, implementation was characterized by a process of mutual adap-tation in which project goals and methods were modified to suit the needs and interests of the local staff and in which the staff changed to meet the requirements of the project. (p. 169)

The point to emphasize is that implementation was success-ful when a genuine exchange occurred—cooperation through mutual adaptation. The program was modified to meet the local needs of teachers and the teachers changed their behavior con-sistent with program goals. McLaughlin suggests that these find-ings are more consistent with a view of implementation that values and allows local discretion. One way to attempt to solve the implementation problem—consistent with the authority paradigm—is to attempt to control the process absolutely. Here, education reform initiatives might place emphasis upon speci-ficity to "minimize the necessity for individual users to make decisions or choices" by creating "'teacher proof' packages" that will "reduce local variability" and create "consistent project out-comes" (p. 178). The alternate view—consistent with the ex-change paradigm—"assumes that local variability is not only inevitable, but a good thing, if a proposed innovation is to result in significant and sustained change" (p. 178).[8] McLaughlin finds value in exchange. Contrary to those who view exchange as disabling to government, she suggests that it is beneficial and provides the basis for the federal government to induce lasting change in local institutions.

Exchange and Implementation Failure

For the exchange paradigm, implementation failure is a result of incompatible interests—conflict—within the implementation process. To analyze implementation from this perspective one must first describe the strategic context in which implementation occurs. Any one of three possible states may exist depending upon the preferences of the implementation participants over the possible outcomes (Oye, 1985). A mixed motive context exists if there are mutual benefits from cooperation—whenever both of the participants favor mutual adaptation to policy stagnation. In this context incentives exist both to cooperate and to defect.[9] If one participant favors policy stagnation to mutual adaptation, the interaction is Deadlock. No feasible solution exists because there is no mutual benefit from cooperation. Harmony is created whenever implementation participants prefer cooperation to defection; cooperation, requiring only the pursuit of self-interest, is not problematic in this context. (These conditions are discussed in more detail in the chapter 3.)

EXCHANGE AND THE IMPLEMENTATION PARADOX

If the implementation process empowers potential adversaries, the exchange paradigm suggests that an accommodation must be achieved or the process will stagnate. Three strategies to avoid the implementation paradox are implied by the exchange paradigm. First, given its emphasis upon the satisfaction of implementation participants, the scope of national policy could be limited to those purposes for which willing partners can be found. This would reduce the national policy agenda to little more than a mirror of the desires and preferences of states and localities or key commercial interests; diffuse authority would be inconsequential as willing partners may be expected to cooperate to implement policy.

The second strategy is to bypass reluctant partners and create pseudomarkets in which the national government may deliver social services by directly empowering consumers. This strategy implies that particular implementation participants are entrenched obstacles to constructive change; however, this strategy may be compromised if conditions are right for market failure—a distinct possibility in many of the contexts in which this solution might be applied.

The third possibility is to undertake programs in which the federal government entices reluctant partners to cooperate by offering rewards and inducements. By providing incentives for cooperation, implementors could perhaps become part of a constructive partnership with federal policy formulators. This suggestion reflects the traditional assumption of "cooperative federalism": It attempts to reduce the problem of cooperation to a balance sheet of benefits and costs. What this approach overlooks is that cooperation from reluctant partners may be little more than symbolic. The federal government is likely to be frustrated in its attempts to buy cooperation, because punishing exploitation would be self-defeating; the federal government enjoys little leverage to assure that its purposes are carried out in exchange for resources provided because the options available to punish exploitation have the effect of precluding the possibility of achieving national policy goals.

CRITICISMS OF THE EXCHANGE PARADIGM

The problem with the exchange paradigm is its lack of clarity about what sorts of compromises legitimately satisfy implementation participants. The paradigm places too much emphasis on the satisfaction of implementation participants. The welfare of others outside the implementation process is a concern mainly when it affects the well-being of well-placed implementors. In matters of policy, the welfare of others—those who are the ostensible beneficiaries of the policy—is, or ought to be, central. The exchange paradigm errs by not asserting that policy ought not to exist solely for the benefit of those who implement it.

The exchange paradigm seems to operate in a moral vacuum. The central values relevant to public decisions are those brought to the process by implementation participants. The policy design decision—to include a participant in the implementation process—seems to offer a license to pursue self-interest: it is power without responsibility. The exchange paradigm is morally flawed because it implies that all aspects of the implementation process are negotiable, regardless of their implications for program performance.

Pushed to its limit, the exchange paradigm implies that participants may act as if the implementation process is a second round of policy formulation in which it is possible to substantially alter or even reverse the outcome of the initial round. This makes it difficult to discern where policy formulation ends and implementation begins (Stone, 1980; Nakamura and Pinderhughes, 1981; Barrett and Hill, 1984). If reformulation of policy occurs during implementation, the political influence of groups may be redistributed quietly, even covertly, to the detriment of democracy (Stone, 1980); the moral authority of public policy initiatives may be undermined (Thompson, 1984); and the ability to evaluate implementation performance, at least by the standards of the instrumental model, evaporates (Sabatier, 1986).

The scope of implementation circumstances that the exchange paradigm can explain is limited, given its emphasis on incompatible interests. Implementation failure is explained by conflict of interest. Implementation success, then, results from compatibility of interests—an absence of conflict. However, the exchange paradigm cannot explain the behavior of implementation participants should they, in the most likely circumstance, have incentives both to cooperate and to defect—a mixed motive context. Why and how mixed motive conflicts are resolved is a question that is beyond the exchange paradigm's scope. No attention is paid to how implementors, in this context, can operate to realize their mutual interests.

The exchange paradigm anticipates cooperation in the implementation process only when it leads to mutual gains for all who have a veto. This implies that the decision rule that governs policy implementation is unanimity—only those policies that have little or no serious opposition can be implemented. This would restrict the possible solutions to national policy problems to two classes: Pareto-preferred solutions—initiatives that make everyone better off—and solutions that include side payments as compensation from those who are enriched from the initiative to those who suffer loss as a consequence of the policy initiative (Pareto's near cousin).

Seen this way, the exchange paradigm is a variant of the disability argument. It is often argued that policy gridlock occurs because available policy alternatives make someone worse off. The process provides numerous opportunities for various interests to seek protection from harm, limiting the policy options of government. As a consequence, serious problems go unsolved and the character of de facto solutions may be troubling. The looming federal budget deficit is an example. The inability of the government to reduce spending or to raise taxes results in inaction that has the effect of pushing the deficit off onto future generations. The implication is that the national government is reduced to "feel-good" policies that involve no sacrifice on the part of constituencies who influence the course of policy.

This is a powerful argument that has much merit. However, it fails to distinguish economic from political relationships. The unique character of political relationships makes cooperation possible even when it imposes direct costs upon individuals who could veto the initiative. Political leadership can, and often does, create circumstances in which citizens, firms, and state and local governments cooperate to achieve public goals despite the intense desire to avoid the costs that such initiatives imply. Beyond this, the exchange paradigm does not consider the possibility that preferences and opinions could change over time in response to public discourse or shifts in perspective that come from realizing the social implications of one's actions. In viewing processes in which public policy is implemented as an amalgamation of "private" decisions, the possibility of increased awareness or development of social consciousness is lost to the exchange paradigm.

The exchange paradigm lacks a normative foundation. It assumes that all values are equally legitimate and diminishes the importance of direction provided by policy formulation. Confusing governance and spontaneous order, the exchange paradigm improperly restricts the scope of public policy to mutually beneficial exchange.

THE NEED FOR A NEW PERSPECTIVE

A new perspective is required if implementation is to be seen as a problem of governance in which cooperation between independent authorities must be induced. In constructing this new perspective the lessons of existing theoretical approaches must be remembered. Following the authority paradigm, implementation must be instrumentally effective and aim to achieve more than the satisfaction of its participants. The exchange paradigm reminds us that federal domination is constrained and emphasizes the positive value of cooperation. However, the exchange paradigm seeks to limit the scope of national policy to matters of consensus; diffuse authority is not problematic when there is an absence of conflict. In so doing, the exchange paradigm overlooks the role of coercive authority in governance. Beyond this, position and strategic options in the implementation process are not givens: these conditions are influenced or created by prior governmental decisions. By contrast, the authority paradigm places too much faith in the coercive authority of government. In viewing federal policy goals as the ultimate expression of value, any and all means are directed to controlling implementation participants. What is needed is an approach that balances concern for instrumental effectiveness with the diffusion of authority characteristic of governance in a liberal, federal polity.

GOVERNANCE

It has been observed that the U.S. government is founded upon liberal, federal principles. This constitutional foundation challenges national leadership by dividing public authority and limiting the scope of government intervention into the market. Vincent Ostrom (1987) has argued that U.S. government is a system of "concurrent jurisdiction." According to Ostrom, the major innovation of U.S. federalist theory was the creation of a "compound republic," consisting of governments of limited scope but general competence (pp. 104–11). Concurrent jurisdiction—the constitution of multiple governments, one national and multiple constituent, each sharing jurisdiction over territory and citizenry—implies the need to cooperate in the implementation of policy, except in those matters in which one government is granted exclusive jurisdiction by the constitution. Ostrom has observed: "Cooperation and coordinated action among various agencies at different levels of government is the hallmark of administration in a federal system. [Hamilton's] emphasis upon cooperation . . . clearly precludes any assumption that American public administration would become a centralized bureaucracy controlled from a single center of authority" (p. 129).

The point of this system of lawmaking and administration is that the execution of national policy would require the construction of compound majorities. It is insufficient, in implementing national policy, to merely gain political support to pass a measure in the Congress. For national policy to be acted upon, the cooperation of other authorities would be required; these authorities, by design, would be subject to different political pressures than those that existed for national policy formulators. This political arrangement was supposed to reduce the possibility that national government would be subject to the undue influence of majority factions.

Ostrom's analysis directly challenges the relevance of the authority paradigm to the U.S. case: "concurrent jurisdiction provides the foundation for a cooperative federalism"; "a federal system of government . . . depends, then, not upon integrated hierarchy of command . . . but upon a variety of different cooperative and joint arrangements" (1987, pp. 129–30). Daniel Elazar concurs with Ostrom on this point: "In a federal system, basic policies are made and implemented through negotiation in some form so that all can share in the system's decision making and executing processes" (1987, p. 6).

But, to establish diffuse authority and the need for cooperation as an implication of constitutional principles does not justify it as a political arrangement (a point that top-down analysts have often made in criticizing bottom-up analysts sympathetic to the value of diffuse authority). Linder and Peters (1987) have argued that some analysts are "accepting an empirical difficulty as a normative statement" and thereby confusing empirical and normative statements to the detriment of theory (pp. 465, 471).

The implementation literature has long recognized that diffuse authority exists in the implementation process and that federalism and liberalism play important roles in creating opportunities for strategic behavior. For example, federalism is important to Martha Derthick's (1972) explanation of the failure of President Johnson's new-towns initiative. Eugene Bardach (1980) has suggested that diffuse authority is pernicious, permitting implementation participants to play "games" that exploit the process. Helen Ingram (1977) and Ripley and Franklin (1982) have described implementation as a bargaining process in which the federal government does not always have the upper hand. Lester Salamon has noted the increased use of "third parties," not always public, who enjoy a "substantial degree of autonomy from Federal control" to implement federal programs (1981, p. 260).

Though diffuse authority is widely observed, implementation analysts are split regarding its implications for governance. To some, diffuse authority is an important political value: Salamon (1981) argued that "the preservation of state and local autonomy are viewed as political values in their own right, worth protecting even at the cost of some sacrifice of administrative efficiency or national purpose." Diffuse authority also has been disparaged: it is a source of destructive games (Bardach, 1980); it enhances bureaucratic influence at the expense of policy formulators (Edwards, 1980); and it is viewed as an inconvenient remnant of a bygone era that must be circumvented or controlled to govern the modern state (Goodnow, 1967). More ominously, diffuse authority may be cast as a bastion of evil and injustice that can reside within a federal system of governance (Riker, 1964; especially the concluding chapter on racism and federalism). In spite of the apparent value Ostrom places in federalism, he has noted that the checks that result from diffuse authority create the potential for stalemate and immobility in government rather than necessarily encouraging thoughtful deliberation and reduction of error (1987, p. 162).

The often implicit point of criticism is that *diffuse authority diminishes the influence of national majorities* (or at least their expression in national policy initiatives). This is taken as an affront to democratic values in public decision making. Consequently, the diffusion of authority implied by federal and liberal principles stands between the federal government and the realization of its view of the national interest, rendering constitutional principles as a disabling force that U.S. national government must strive to overcome.

Hayek (1960) provides a partial answer to this criticism. Observing that in democratic government legislative authority is subordinate to constitutional authority, he states: "a constitutional system does not involve an absolute limitation of the will of the people but merely a subordination of immediate objectives to long-term ones" (p. 180). The tendency of implementation analysts has been to focus upon immediate objectives and to view constitutional values as contextual features—expressions of political value, institutional constraints, or needless impediments to policy success.

Hayek's point, applied directly to the issue at hand, implies that the political power of reluctant partners—their institutional role in the implementation process—represents a long-term objective of the polity. That serving this long-term objective should from time-to-time frustrate attempts to achieve immediate policy objectives is not a circumvention of popular will but a triumph of principle over expediency. But principle has its price. Hayek (1960) observes: "It is inevitable that, by accepting general principles, they will tie their hands as far as particular issues are concerned" (p. 181).

Hayek argues that the frustration of immediate objectives may be seen as an illustration of the governing process at work, not the failure of government. This is a compelling counterpoint to the implicit premise of much of the implementation literature—that a failure to complete an announced policy is prima facie evidence of implementation failure. If implementation is part of the governing process, outcomes that imply no change in policy—literal implementation failures—cannot be routinely interpreted as failures of governance. Consider for example, former president Reagan's oft-proposed policy to fight the "war on drugs" by conducting, without cause, drug tests in the federal workplace—an apt example of the subordination of constitutional principles to immediate policy goals. Is nonimplementation of this policy evidence of a failure of U.S. government or an illustration of the process at work?

Seen another way, Hayek's argument is a restatement of the disability thesis—the view that U.S. government is disabled by design. The United States' government is constrained by its own formative principles—federalism and liberalism make national leadership a difficult, if not impossible, task. Hayek's point may be to clarify the disability argument—failures to act do not necessarily constitute failures to govern. But, to claim that immediate policy objectives must sometimes be sacrificed for principle is an important, but incomplete, response to critics of diffuse authority. It properly suggests that effective governance of a liberal, federal polity cannot be based merely upon expediency—principles matter—but it fails to address the natural concern of the ability of government in such a constitutional system to achieve its policy aims.

Though Hayek (1960) reflects the disability argument, he seeks to persuade the reader that a disabled government may still be a good government. But, with mounting evidence of the existence of serious social problems, the inability of government to act becomes a proper matter of concern. When government responds to problems ineffectually, concern about constitutional principles may seem out of balance with concern about getting the job done. Does a society constituted on the basis of diffuse authority—liberalism and federalism—jeopardize hope for effective governance? If not, what are the principles of effective governance in a condition of diffuse authority?

Cooperation and Governance

Theories of federal administration (cf. Ostrom, 1987; Elazar, 1987) suggest that cooperation is the key to implementing national policy. But if constitutional principles introduce reluctant partners into the implementation process, an environment for collective decision making is created that is laden with conflict. If conflict diminishes the likelihood of cooperation, the administrative foundation that Ostrom and Elazar seek for effective government is undermined: the implementation process becomes a paradox and national policy falls under its own weight.

However, the implementation paradox is a reflection of the dominant views of the implementation process: It reflects the authority paradigm's concerns for comprehensive federal control of the implementation process, and it reflects the belief of the exchange paradigm that only matters of policy without significant conflict may be implemented in a context of diffuse authority. Much of the concern regarding the effectiveness of federal administration is a result of the introduction of conflict by reluctant partners brought into the implementation process.

Is this concern misplaced? Is the direct equation of conflict with a tendency to resist cooperation faulty?

Theories of conflict resolution link the extent of conflict in collective decision making to the likelihood of cooperation (see, for example, Axelrod, 1970). However, the two are conceptually separate. Cooperation is more properly seen as a response to conflict, not the absence of it (Axelrod, 1984). Beyond this, outcomes to strategic interactions are only unambiguously predicted in the relatively rare cases of Harmony and Deadlock. The outcome of the more likely strategic context—any one of many possible mixed motive games—is viewed as ambiguous.

This implies that while the strategic context is important, it is often not the determining factor in decisions to cooperate. Although there is a wide range of ambiguity regarding the effect of conflict upon the likelihood of cooperation in a mixed motive context, theories of cooperation suggest that the likelihood of cooperation can be altered even when the amount of conflict is held constant. This implies that the problem is not to eliminate all conflict—the false hope of the exchange paradigm—but instead to create conditions in which participants are more likely to respond to conflict with cooperation.

Hayek's point that constitutional principles may impede progress on specific issues—and more significantly the disability thesis—is relevant not whenever conflict exists in the implementation process, but whenever cooperation cannot be induced as a response to conflict—the empowerment of reluctant partners is disabling only when it undermines cooperation. The flaw in the disability thesis, and the implementation literature that reflects it, is that it may be possible to manipulate the conditions of the implementation process to encourage cooperative responses to conflicts of interest. This possibility has received scant attention in the literature.

CONCLUSION

The foundation upon which the implementation literature has been built is that government power is created by legislative initiative, only later to be diluted during the implementation process. An alternative view was suggested in the first chapter. From this perspective, the power to govern emerges from the creation of arrangements which allow those who control resources to cooperate in pursuit of collective goals. During the implementation process the power to govern may be generated. If governance is creating the "capacity to act" (Stone, 1989), bringing together the resources required to accomplish the collective ends of society, a new perspective on political leadership in a liberal, federal polity is implied. Reluctant partners do not disable national government, they generate the power to govern within a structure of constitutional representation of interest. Bringing reluctant partners into the implementation process need not dilute federal power; it may be the means by which the power to govern is realized. From this perspective, government that must work in a context of diffuse authority is not necessarily disabled, but it is dependent upon sources of political power that are not rooted exclusively in authority. Political leadership must generate the capacity to govern by seeking constructive cooperation from others.[10]

The implementation paradox can now be resolved. Implementation analysis that begins with the assumption that shared power is diluted power must lead to the paradox. However, the paradox is resolved when one realizes that the inclusion of reluctant partners in the implementation process generates power and the ability to govern. To understand the problem of governing a liberal, federal polity one must first examine the problems of coordinating the activities of independent actors: How can independent authorities be motivated to cooperate in achieving public goals despite the absence of a dominating authority?

3 IMPLEMENTATION REGIMES

IN A FEDERAL polity with a liberal political economy, policy-relevant authority is fragmented. Consequently, national policy initiatives are implemented in a tense environment: tension exists between the desires to maintain a diffuse distribution of authority consistent with constitutional principles and to enjoy the benefits of scale, cost sharing, consistency, and coordination that may be found in national policy initiatives.

When authority is fragmented, the challenge of national governance is to induce cooperation and policy coordination among independent authorities. Governance is not "a task of comprehensive control," but a "bringing together of essential elements in an otherwise fragmented world" (Stone, 1989, p. 227). But how can cooperation be induced when implementation participants are self-interested and autonomous?

Theories of conflict resolution suggest that the likelihood of cooperative behavior is linked to the degree of conflict of interest between participants in a collective decision (Axelrod, 1970). However, it may not always be possible to avoid or reduce conflict. When the degree of conflict of interest cannot be reduced, theories of cooperation and regime development suggest contextual conditions and policy actions that increase the probability of cooperation and policy coordination through mutual adaptation (Axelrod, 1984; Oye, 1985; Axelrod and Keohane, 1985). In this chapter, theoretical insights developed in the fields of conflict resolution, regime development, and cooperation theory are applied to the problems of implementing national policy.

THE REGIME PERSPECTIVE

From the perspective of the implementation regime framework, the implementation process is a strategic interaction; participants enjoy substantial autonomy but, because of interdependence, must cooperate to achieve their ends. Strategic behavior during the implementation process may take two forms. When participation is mandatory, strategic behavior is a change in practice that circumvents or mitigates the effect of federal policy demands. When participation in federal policy is voluntary, the definition of strategic behavior is expanded to include nonparticipation.

The possibility of strategic behavior makes the realization of cooperation problematic; participants have incentives to exploit the cooperative behavior of others. In order to implement its policies, the federal government must establish a context in which implementation participants are likely to cooperate in pursuit of national policy goals. Regime analysis examines the implementation process to determine whether context or mechanisms exist to promote cooperation and policy coordination. Two essential contextual elements are: strategic context (indicated by the degree of conflict between participants in the interaction) and institutional context (mechanisms or arrangements in the implementation process that encourage cooperation).

Although implementation occurs within an established system of governance, the regime framework assumes that cooperation must be nurtured within the implementation process. This assumption challenges notions of "cooperative federalism" that date to the founders of the United States. Vincent Ostrom (1987, p. 129) observes that Alexander Hamilton stated "the basic premise for a cooperative federalism" in *The Federalist*. Commenting on the possibility of policy coordination between the national and state governments in matters of taxation, Hamilton asserted: "As neither can *control* the other each will have an obvious and sensible interest in this reciprocal forbearance. And where there is an *immediate* common interest, we may safely count upon its operation." (Rossiter, 1961, p. 221, emphasis in the original).

The premise of cooperative federalism, reflected in Hamilton's assertion, is that mutual interest is a sufficient condition for policy coordination in a federal system of governance. Theories of conflict resolution support the claim that mutual interest is necessary for cooperation, but mutual interest alone is no guarantee. The assumption that mutual interest is sufficient to induce cooperation must be reexamined in light of theory regarding the problems of cooperation and policy coordination between independent actors. Mancur Olson states that the provision of public goods is problematic, even in the face of mutual interest (1971). Garrett Hardin has argued that some problems—specifically the tragedy of the commons—defy resolution by the rational calculations of individuals (1977).

In a mixed motive context, incentives to exploit the cooperative behavior of others can make it difficult to realize cooperation. To overcome this difficulty, the regime literature identifies contextual conditions that facilitate the development of cooperation between autonomous actors. Cooperation is more likely when participants are engaged in an ongoing relationship that creates a record of constructive interaction and expectations for the future. When these conditions are absent, unilateral actions may be undertaken by implementation participants to enhance the possibilities for cooperation. Possible actions include issue linkage, establishing rules of conduct, boosting the rewards of cooperation, and dividing programs into a series of smaller exchanges (Axelrod, 1984; Oye, 1985). To arrange aspects of the implementation process so as to induce cooperation in the face of conflicting interests is what we shall call the design and development of an implementation regime.

IMPLEMENTATION REGIMES

A regime is a political arrangement that institutionalizes values important in public decision making; but a regime is also a set of organizational arrangements that helps to define and support the political values inherent in it.[1] Thus, an *implementation regime* can be an arrangement among implementation participants that identifies the values to be served during the implementation process and provides an organizational framework to promote those values.

At the organizational level, a regime is a system of rules, norms, and procedures that governs the interaction of participants in some collective decision. The regime may alter the costs of transactions, availability of information, or level of uncertainty in the decision process (Axelrod and Keohane, 1985); it may promote cooperation by making the relationship between participants more regular and predictable. The political context in which implementation occurs is largely defined by the regime's organizational arrangements: Who is positioned to influence the outcome of the implementation process? Who should be consulted (and in what circumstances)? What information is shared with whom? What are the standards of acceptable behavior? How will standards and procedures be enforced?

Regimes are shaped by "potentially conflicting principles" that seek to guide public decision making (Stone, 1987, p. 269). A federalist regime, for example, must reconcile the conflicting desires for central leadership and diffuse implementation authority. This problem is characteristic of policy proposals generated by the national government of a federal polity with a liberal political economy. To implement policy, a governing arrangement must be created that joins the means and ends of the implementation process.

Many important aspects of the implementation regime framework have been drawn from the literature on international cooperation (see, for example, Young, 1980; Keohane, 1984; Oye, 1985; Axelrod and Keohane, 1985).[2] That literature views international policy coordination as a strategic problem; independent authorities must cooperate to realize their mutual interests, despite varying perceptions and interests, uncertainty, and shared authority. The implementation regime framework projects this problem to the implementation of national policies in a liberal, federal context; intergovernmental or cross-sectoral policy implementation requires cooperation. However, when constitutional principles demand diffuse authority, tension is created during the implementation process that is not easily overcome, challenging leadership from the national government and even complicating the implementation of policies that promise mutual gains.

THE CREATION OF REGIMES

Oran Young (1982) has identified three ways in which international regimes are likely to develop, two of which are relevant to the creation of implementation regimes. Some international regimes spring from spontaneous order. Following Hayek's definition (see the discussion in chapter 2), regimes of this sort evolve from the regular, uncoordinated actions of independent actors seeking their own ends. International regimes also may develop through a processes of deliberate negotiation. In this case, parties with mutual interests would organize to realize the benefits that can come from exchange within an explicit framework. Finally, international regimes may be imposed by force or coercion. Imposed regimes are based upon coercive power, the ability of one actor to enhance or threaten the well-being of another.

Not all of these means of regime creation are relevant to the implementation of national policy within an established system of governance. The two exceptions distinguish the creation of implementation regimes: (1) spontaneous order cannot be a source of implementation regimes; (2) the forms of coercive power relevant to implementation regimes are somewhat different.

A regime that springs from spontaneous order cannot be regarded as a foundation for an implementation regime because such an order does not attempt to accomplish a specific end. Implementation regimes must be rooted in policy—an intentional intervention by those who hold positions of political authority. Spontaneous order is not a policy but an absence of policy. (Note that this exclusion does not prevent the use of marketlike mechanisms to implement policy. Even when policy is implemented using marketlike structures, the organizational ideal of spontaneous order, goal-oriented intervention by public authority has occurred.) Because spontaneous order lacks a goal-oriented intervention by public authority, it lacks the instrumental element that is essential to implementation regimes. Coercive power relevant to the formulation of implementation regimes, because it is exercised within established systems of governance, is likely to be of a different, less violent kind than that sometimes applied in the international arena. Coercion within established governance is likely to occur within a legal framework that specifies impermissible behavior and prescribes specific penalties for noncompliance. Most implementation regimes are formed through a combination of negotiation and imposition.

The Fort Lincoln new town example (discussed in chapter 1) could be interpreted as an attempt to establish a negotiated regime. In that case, local officials were subjected to pressures from federal officials and specific consideration was offered as a condition for cooperation in pursuit of the federal policy objective. However, in another sense, the regime was imposed because its creation, though not its final form, was a result of actions taken by authorities external to local intermediaries in the implementation process.

But how relevant is coercive authority? If diffuse authority implies the ability to veto policy, isn't it possible to avoid or mitigate the effects of coercion, as in the Fort Lincoln case? If so, is national government limited to those few policy initiatives that are Pareto-preferred? To accept this view is to overlook the unique character of public authority—its legitimate use of coercion. But what is the role of coercion in inducing cooperation?

Coercion and Cooperation

Coercion can play a role in inducing cooperation; it can compel implementors to participate and, by manipulating the consequences of performance, even perhaps providing penalties for noncompliance or rewards for cooperation, coercive power can alter the incentives of implementation participants and the strategic context in which implementation occurs. However, there are four reasons why coercion alone is often unable to induce cooperation. First, coercion is costly because its operation requires regular monitoring of performance and enforcement. Enforcement is costly in two ways: There are operational costs and opportunity costs. The operational costs of coercion can be extensive when one considers the scope of national policy initiatives and the extent of effort required to check compliance with federal directives. However, opportunity costs may be even more vexing. When the federal government seeks cooperation in pursuit of its policy goals, the most effective available penalty is to withhold resources from the offending party. Often, enforcement of this penalty has the effect of making it impossible to realize the purpose of national policy.

A second reason to doubt the efficacy of coercion is that authority to enforce coercion is always incomplete. As policy is implemented, unforeseen circumstances arise and strategic opportunities are created. When this occurs, coercion can be undermined as rules, performance requirements, or legal sanctions become counterproductive. In this context, the implementation process can quickly degenerate into a series of actions aimed at creating an airtight system of control and counteractions aimed at circumventing it. Third, coercion may alienate implementation participants, fueling the very sorts of behavior it seeks to prevent. Finally, federal policy formulators—congressional representatives in particular—may have little stomach for use of coercive power. Their interest in "cooperative" relationships between federal authorities and their constituents is likely to limit the occasions deemed appropriate for such action. What happens as a consequence is that policy tends to evolve into more distributive forms, in response to political demands, using positive incentives rather than penalties to gain compliance (Sabatier and Mazmanian, 1983). For these reasons, coercion is usually insufficient as a basis for inducing cooperation in a context of diffuse authority.

The Role of Policy Formulation

From the regime perspective, the formulation of national policy initiatives is a declaration of intention. This declaration is important for several reasons: (1) it can structure the expectations of implementors; (2) it can mobilize potential implementation participants or their clients; (3) it can legitimize claims on public resources; (4) it can empower some by designating them as implementation participants; (5) it can distribute public resources; and (6) it may, by committing the federal government to particular outcomes, effect the probability that particular outcomes occur.

However, a declaration of intention—even federal intention backed by substantial resources—is an insufficient foundation on which to govern. The generation of policy initiatives usually does not provide a plan to integrate fragmented elements directed toward a common end. In many cases, the effect of policy formulation is to create tension, institutionalize it, or rearrange the institutional landscape on which it exists. Consequently, with regard to the proper governing arrangement for policy implementation, participants are likely to receive ambiguous signals from policy formulators. This is true even if policy formulators are quite clear and specific about the policy's objective.

Policy initiatives structure and influence the character of implementation regimes. However, the possibilities for regime development are not limited to what is specified by the policy initiative. Reflecting patterns Young (1982) has observed in the international arena, it is possible that governing arrangements can be formally negotiated during the implementation process or that a regime will emerge gradually as the practices of implementation participants and their patterns of interaction become regular. In this way, the possibilities for change and development in the relationships between implementation participants and the importance of implementation activities is greater than the existing theories of the implementation process would suggest.

The formulation of policy influences the development of regimes by positioning interests and distributing resources. This has substantial influence over the strategic context in which implementation occurs. However, the formulation of policy is usually insufficient in resolving conflicts of interest, leaving the problem of inducing cooperation to implementation participants. How then can cooperation be induced?

ELABORATING THE REGIME FRAMEWORK

Strategic and institutional context influence the inclination of implementation participants to cooperate. To understand this influence, it is necessary to elaborate on the implementation regime framework. A satisfactory basis from which to begin is the reciprocal decision process presented in the discussion of the exchange paradigm (see figure 1). Although there is an apparent kinship between the exchange paradigm and the regime framework, an important distinction exists: the regime framework is oriented specifically to the strategic context that is ambiguous from the perspective of the exchange paradigm, situations of mixed motives. In a mixed motive interaction incentives exist both to cooperate and to defect. Although there are mutual benefits from cooperation, there are also incentives to exploit the cooperative behavior of others.

From the regime perspective, conflict resolution is a key aspect of the implementation process. However, the nature of the strategic problem is conceived broadly to include difficulties that exist in the realization of cooperation. To be clear, cooperation must be distinguished from the absence of conflict. Robert Keohane (1984) has described cooperation as negotiation to bring separate entities into conformity with one another; this highly political activity can occur only when actors adjust their behavior to the actual or anticipated behavior of others (p. 53). Paradoxically, cooperation, as defined here, can occur only when the interests of implementation participants are in conflict.

Understanding the mixed motive strategic context helps to further clarify the nature of reluctant partners—they are implementation participants in a mixed motive game; that is, implementors who experience cross pressures to cooperate and to defect within a game created by policy formulators. Consequently, the cooperation of implementors is uncertain and may be difficult to achieve. As we shall see, this definition implies restrictions on the nature of preferences that participants may have over the outcomes of the game.

Two conditions are required for a mixed motive game.[3] First, there must be some benefit from cooperation; this means that all participants must prefer mutual cooperation (CC) to mutual defection (DD). Second, for coordination of choice to be necessary to realize mutual benefits, unilateral defection (DC) must be preferred to unrequited cooperation (CD) (these conditions are discussed in Oye, 1985). If the first condition is violated, that is, if one actor prefers stalemate (DD) to cooperation (CC), the interaction is stillborn in Deadlock and implementors are not reluctant partners because there is no incentive to cooperate. If the second condition is violated, that is, if one actor prefers unrequited cooperation (CD) to unilateral defection (DC), Harmony exists and implementors are willing —not reluctant—partners who may realize cooperation without coordination simply by pursuing their individual self-interest. This distinction between these classes of games suggests that a relationship exists between strategic context and the likelihood of cooperation.

CONFLICT AND COOPERATION

In his work on conflict resolution, Robert Axelrod (1970) explored the relationship between the level of conflict of interest between participants in a mixed motive decision and their inclination to cooperate. His models of strategic interaction suggest that an inverse relationship exists between the level of conflict of interest and the likelihood of cooperation.

Axelrod developed a method to estimate the level of conflict in a given strategic interaction. He accomplished this by normalizing the payoffs the players associate with each outcome.[4] When the utility payoffs are graphed and joined by line segments, they form a region within which agreement is feasible (this entire region is within the unit square). The area northeast of this region, but still within the unit square, is the conflict zone. To measure the amount of conflict, calculate the area of the region in the conflict zone and compare it to the total area of the unit square. The result is an estimate of the amount of conflict of interest from 0.0 to 0.5. The greater the amount of conflict the greater the likelihood of conflictual behavior.

Consider an example to clarify Axelrod's method. A game in which the conflict of interest is at its maximum is the "dollar division game." In this game (presented in figure 2), two participants must agree on the division of a dollar. If no agreement is reached, the payoff for each is zero. Feasible demands for each participant include a range from having the entire dollar for themselves to getting nothing. These demands may be represented as a mixed motive game given the following preference orderings of the participants:

Players 1 & 2 DC > CC > CD or DD

When the payoffs are normalized the game may be presented

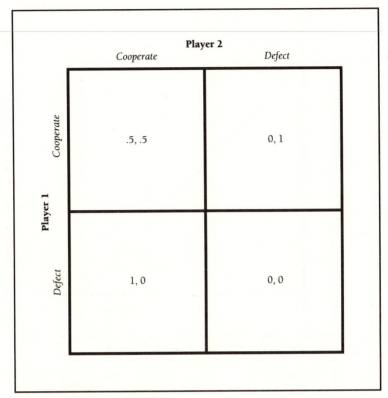

FIG. 2. Dollar Division Game

in graphic form as in figure 3. Note that conflict of interest is at its maximum value (0.5). This result is developed from a comparison of the area of the conflict zone to the unit square. Now, consider Axelrod's (1970) claim that reductions in the amount of conflict of interest make cooperation more likely. To assess this claim, compare the game in figure 3 to an alternative game in which the conflict of interest has been reduced (presented in graphic form in figure 4). In figure 4 a new compromise outcome has been identified, causing the region within which agreement is feasible to protrude into the conflict zone. This means that this game has less conflict of interest than ex-

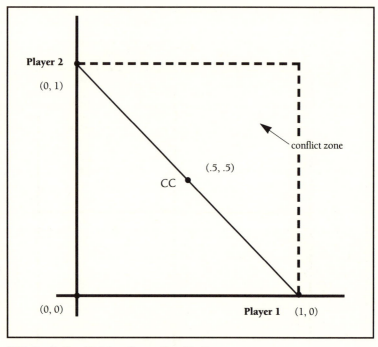

FIG. 3. Dollar Division Game, Graphic Form

isted in the dollar division game (the exact amount of the reduction depends upon the payoffs-associated compromise and
is not important to this line of argument). Has this reduction in
conflict of interest made participants more inclined to cooperate?
If participants are expected-value decision makers, it follows
that the probability of cooperation increases as the expected
value of outcomes associated with cooperation increase. The
shift from CC to CC′ represents just such a change, indicating
that an implication of Axelrod's (1970) model is that as conflict
of interest declines, the likelihood of cooperation increases.

There are a variety of different types of mixed motive games,
each distinguished from the others on the basis of the participants' preference orderings over the possible outcomes. Though
these games share defining characteristics, distinctions between

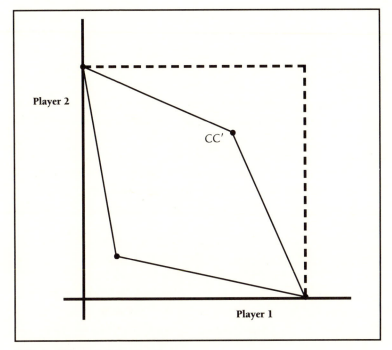

FIG. 4. Prisoner's Dilemma Game

the various types are important for the influence that Axelrod (1970) has suggested exists between the level of conflict and the incentives for cooperation.

THE PRISONER'S DILEMMA

Perhaps the most familiar mixed motive game is the Prisoner's Dilemma. The game is often illustrated by a story of two prisoners arrested as suspected accomplices in crime. Although there is compelling evidence of minor offenses, the evidence for prosecution on more serious charges is weak. The police separate the suspects and offer each the opportunity to confess, implicating the other, in exchange for a lighter sentence. If one alone confesses, he receives a lighter sentence while the other is prosecuted on the more serious charges. If both confess, they are sentenced for more serious crimes than would be possible if both were to remain silent. Each must decide whether to remain silent (cooperate) or confess (defect).

The game presented in figure 4 is a Prisoner's Dilemma. In the figure, the points on the graph are indications only of the order in which the preferences of the participants are expressed—magnitude is not relevant when the game is played only once. It is further assumed in this presentation that the game is symmetric—that is, it looks the same to both players and so assignment of the players to a particular axis is not important.

The Prisoner's Dilemma game may be described formally by the following preference ordering for each player: DC > CC > DD > CD. For each player, the most preferred outcome is unilateral defection (to exploit the other suspect, implicating him in exchange for a lighter sentence). Following this, joint cooperation (both remain silent) is preferred to mutual defection (both confess). The least preferred outcome is unrequited cooperation—being played as a "sucker" (to be implicated by the other while remaining silent). When the game is iterated—played numerous times—an additional condition is required regarding the magnitude of differences between the outcomes: CC must be greater than DC-CD. This means that for the game to be a Prisoner's Dilemma, the payoff value of mutual cooperation must exceed the value it is possible for participants to achieve if they take turns exploiting each other.

Of the mixed motive games to be considered here, the Prisoner's Dilemma is that in which players are least likely to engage in cooperative behavior. Players in the noniterated version of this game have a dominant strategy—one which leads them to their best possible outcome regardless of the decision of the other player—to defect. Each participant has this incentive because, in so doing, he precludes the possibility of being a sucker (the worst possible outcome) and opens the possibility of exploitation, the best possible outcome. The play of the dominant strategies by each participant results in outcome DD (both confess). This outcome is an equilibrium point; an outcome which has a certain sort of stability because neither participant would unilaterally abandon it. Of course, the dilemma is that the players' pursuit of individual self-interest leads both to the equilibrium outcome, mutual defection (DD); an outcome that is less preferable than mutual cooperation (CC).

The Prisoner's Dilemma game expresses an essential problem of cooperation; it is a strategic context in which the pursuit of individual self-interest leads to collective disaster. Extended beyond the two-person case, the problem of cooperation expressed by Prisoner's Dilemma becomes the tragedy of the commons (see Hardin and Baden, 1977).

> Picture a pasture open to all. It is to be expected that each herdsman will try to keep as many cattle as possible on the commons. . . . As a rational being, each herdsman seeks to maximize his gain . . . the rational herdsman concludes that the only sensible course for him to pursue is to add another animal to the herd. . . . But this conclusion is reached by each and every rational herdsman sharing a commons. Therein is the tragedy. Each man is locked in a system that compels him to increase his herd without limit—in a world that is limited. Ruin is the destination toward which all men rush, each pursuing his own best interest in a society that believes in the freedom of the commons. Freedom in a commons brings ruin to all. (Hardin, 1977, p. 20)

The immediate lesson of the Prisoner's Dilemma is that strategic context matters. In some circumstances, the pursuit of self-interest can lead to collective problems in spite of benefits from mutual cooperation. If possible, this strategic context should be avoided. But what if it is not possible to manipulate the strategic context? Is all hope of cooperation lost? To move from the equilibrium point, the prisoners must coordinate their choices to avoid an outcome which both agree is suboptimal. How can the participants coordinate their choices to receive the value of cooperation?

In some circumstances, it is not possible to do so. When a Prisoner's Dilemma game is played only once, when communication is not allowed, and when agreements cannot be enforced, self-interested players must confront the dilemma that rationality leads them to a suboptimal outcome. To some, notably Garrett Hardin (1977), this problem is so compelling that it calls for creation of a Leviathan.[5] Many in the implementation literature, as indicated by the extensive application of the authority paradigm, favor this sort of solution. However, such a strong central authority is inconsistent with the principles that underlie U.S. government. Is authority the only solution? Theories of cooperation and regime development suggest that manipulation of the conditions in which Prisoner's Dilemma (and other mixed motive games) occurs, especially if opportunities for reciprocity between participants can be created, can help to induce cooperation in a context of diffuse authority.

OTHER MIXED MOTIVE GAMES

Several other types of mixed motive games exist. If the preferences of the participants over the outcomes of the interaction are changed, the Prisoner's Dilemma may be transformed into another type of mixed motive interaction. When the CC (mutual cooperation) point moves to the northeast of the DC point for each participant, indicating an increase in the value of mutual cooperation, the Prisoner's Dilemma is transformed into a Stag Hunt game (see figure 5). Oye (1985) has described this game:

> A group of hunters surround a stag. If all cooperate to trap the stag, all will eat well (CC). If one person defects to chase a passing rabbit, the stag will escape. The defector will eat lightly (DC) and none of the others will eat at all (CD). If all chase rabbits, all will have some chance of catching a rabbit and eating lightly (DD). Each hunter's preference ordering is: CC > DC > DD > CD. The mutual interest in plentiful venison (CC)

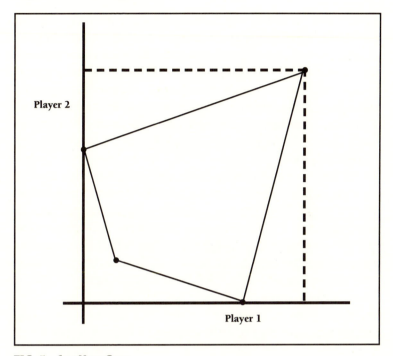

FIG. 5. Stag Hunt Game

relative to all other outcomes militates strongly against defection. However, because a rabbit in the hand (DC) is better than a stag in the bush (CD), cooperation will be assured only if each hunter believes that all hunters will cooperate." (P. 8)

The public accommodations requirements of the Civil Rights Act of 1964 offer a more realistic illustration. Hotel and restaurant owners may be inclined to open their businesses to all, but only if others do so as well. (They may favor cooperation but fear exploitation by those who resist.) The legal requirement becomes a way to assure that all will comply with an action that each agrees is desirable. In spite of having no conflict of interest by Axelrod's (1970) measure, strategic problems exist.

When the strategic context in which implementation occurs

is the Stag Hunt, the essential task of the implementation regime is to assure participants that others are not likely to be tempted to defect. When translated into administrative concerns this means that the regime must specify the terms of cooperative behavior and create transparent reporting requirements that reveal the steps required to cooperate. No monumental change in the nature of program administration is required. The filing of action plans, program outlines, or reports are well-established means to this end.

Another sort of mixed motive game is created when the DD point in the Prisoner's Dilemma game is moved to the southwest. What effect does this change have upon the problem of inducing cooperation? When the DD point is located in the space southwest of the CD point for each participant, the strategic context has become a Chicken game.

Chicken was illustrated in a scene from *Rebel Without a Cause*. Referred to as a "chickie run" in the film, James Dean and Buzz speed in stolen cars side-by-side toward a bluff. The first to leap from his car is the chicken. The incentive for each is a mixture of motivations—to avoid the stigma of being the chicken (by not jumping too soon) but also to survive the game (by not jumping too late). The preference orderings of the players in this game are: DC > CC > CD > DD. Each player's first preference is to win (DC), to be the second to leap safely from his car, making the opponent the chicken. Their second preference is to jump simultaneously from the cars (CC)—the contest is a draw and each of the participants enjoys the status that comes from playing a daring game. Their third preference is to be the chicken (CD). Their least preferred outcome is mutual defection, where both plunge over the cliff (DD) (see figure 6).

One important difference between the Chicken game and Prisoner's Dilemma is that defection is no longer a dominant strategy. There is danger that if both participants play the defection strategy (or stick with it long enough), seeking to win the game, the game will end in tragedy. Of course, James Dean jumps and survives the chickie run. Brushing dust from his pants, he asks, "Where's Buzz?" Buzz has been busy providing

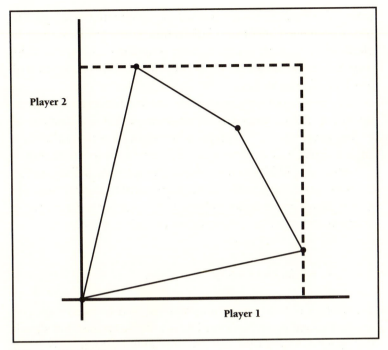

FIG. 6. Chicken Game

a dramatic lesson in the limits of rational decision making by driving off the bluff to his death; unable to stop the speeding car in time, he cannot jump when the strap of his black leather jacket becomes caught on the door handle.

How does this change in the game affect the likelihood of cooperation? Movement of the mutual defection point represents a change in the incentive that participants have to defect. When the game is Chicken, each participant prefers to be exploited rather than to suffer the consequences of mutual defection. The fear of mutual defection, when policy stagnation makes everyone worse off, diminishes incentives to defect. But a strategic problem remains: How to avoid exploitation?

In the strategic context of the Chicken game, the implementation regime must address the problem of assuring participants that each is moving toward the cooperative strategy. The terms of what constitutes satisfactory cooperation should be clarified along with a specific plan to achieve that end. In this way, participants can move to coordinate their strategies with less fear of exploitation.

Of course, the outcome of the interaction may not be co-operative. Participants may attempt to exploit one another by exchanging threats. The player who can make a commitment to such a threat and communicate this intention to his adversary can effectively blackmail the other participant (Schelling, 1970). Blackmail may be feasible in the implementation process if one participant is more committed (due to resource investments or political demands) to continuation of the program.

TACIT BARGAINING

Techniques of tacit bargaining may be used to induce cooper-ation in mixed motive games. This subject—applied specifically to Prisoner's Dilemma—was explored in Robert Axelrod's work, *The Evolution of Cooperation* (1984). Axelrod asks the question central to this discussion: "Under what conditions will coop-eration emerge in a world of egoists without central authority?" (p. 3). To address this question, Axelrod reports the perfor-mance of various strategic options played in computerized game tournaments. The most effective strategy was Tit-for-Tat: begin with cooperation and then, without exception, play whatever the opponent played in the preceding round. This strategy pros-pered "not by beating the other player, but by eliciting behavior from the other player which allowed both to do well" (p. 112).

What are the qualities of this strategy that make it so effec-tive? Axelrod (1984, pp. 36–54) has proposed several charac-teristics of Tit-for-Tat that account for its effectiveness. Tit-for-Tat is a "nice" strategy, never is it the first to defect. It is "retaliatory," defecting immediately in response to a defection from the opponent. It is "forgiving," switching to cooperation as soon as the opponent does. Tit-for-Tat has "clarity": it can be easily identified by other strategies. It is "robust": the strategy does well against many others.

The results of the game tournament suggest ways to induce cooperation through tacit bargaining. Axelrod (1984, pp. 126–41) suggests several ways to induce cooperation in an iterated Prisoner's Dilemma game. One is to "enlarge the shadow of the future"; that is, to cause participants to make decisions in the present in anticipation of their consequences for the future. When the shadow of the future is enlarged, cooperation becomes more stable because players seek to avoid self-destructive spirals of conflict through mutual defection. Each player avoids the temptation to defect in recognition of the fact that it may damage the long-term relationship.

A second way to induce cooperation is to change the payoffs of the game. If Prisoner's Dilemma could be transformed into some other sort of game, the temptation to defect may be reduced as the value of mutual cooperation or the danger of mutual defection is enhanced. A third way to encourage cooperation is to promote altruism and reciprocity; "teach people to care about the welfare of others" (Axelrod, 1984, p. 134),[6] but recognize that unconditional cooperation is a poor strategy because it can promote exploitation. Finally, the prospects for cooperation are improved when participants have well-developed recognition abilities; the ability to create a sound record of past interactions and to discover the patterns that may exist is an important precondition to recognition that is possible with careful record-keeping and analysis of past experience.

INDUCING COOPERATION IN THE IMPLEMENTATION PROCESS

The problem for implementation participants is in cooperating to achieve common goals despite conflicting interests. The preceding discussion has suggested that cooperative behavior is more likely when participants create a "shadow of the future" (Axelrod, 1984; Oye, 1985). How can this be done within the implementation process? In part, expectations for the future can be created when grand programs are broken down into a series of smaller exchanges, reducing the gain from exploitation and the risk of cooperation. When this is not possible, regime theory suggests that two contextual factors are especially important: (1) a history of interaction between the participants and (2) the expectation of future interaction.

A history of interaction allows each participant to anticipate the consequences of cooperation based upon experience. Beyond this, more or less explicit procedures for reconciling disputes are likely to have developed to serve as conflict mitigation mechanisms. The expectation of ongoing interaction makes exploitive behavior less attractive because it offers opportunities for retaliation. Ongoing interaction also facilitates bargaining and exchange on individual issues as consideration in one case can be linked to reciprocity in another.

When historical experience is lacking or when prospects for the future are unknown, the regime framework suggests several ways for policy formulators or implementation participants to improve the prospects for cooperation and mutual adaptation. Axelrod (1984) suggests that an effective way to foster cooperation is to boost the reward that participants receive: This could be viewed as a side-payment to settle disputes between implementation participants (following the discussion of Pareto's near cousin and the exchange paradigm in chapter 2). To overcome resistance to the costs of implementing policy, contingent rewards may be offered in other, related areas. Another way to alter the expected payoffs of implementation participants is to create issue linkages; arrangements that link the consequences of cooperation in one context to the interests of that party in another (Axelrod and Keohane, 1985). This may reward participants for cooperation or threaten their interests to induce cooperation.

Implementation participants could foster cooperation by developing mechanisms (formal institutions or less formal norms) to make behavior more predictable and constrained. One means to this end is to clarify "standards of conduct," defining cooperative and uncooperative behavior (Oye, 1985). This strategy makes unintended defection less likely and clarifies the expectations of both parties. When rules or mechanisms exist to control conflict, the scope of conflict is limited and predictable, helping to maintain cooperation and avoid conflict by anticipating its sources.

Finally, cooperation may be encouraged by the commitment of one or more parties to the program. One effective way to accomplish this is to guarantee dedicated resources, demonstrating commitment by risking the loss of resources that are not easily transferred to another purpose (Axelrod, 1984; Oye, 1985; Axelrod and Keohane, 1985).

ILLUSTRATING THE REGIME FRAMEWORK

The regime framework can be illustrated briefly by reinterpreting a classic case from the implementation literature, the Oakland initiative undertaken by the Economic Development Administration (EDA). The regime framework offers two possible interpretations of Pressman and Wildavsky's (1983) case. Which one is more accurate depends upon the strategic context that existed, and the evidence is ambiguous. In a mixed motive context, implementation failure is a lost opportunity attributed to the inability of the participants to negotiate effectively. This implies that exchange would have benefited both parties, but the participants were unable to realize their mutual interests. This interpretation is consistent with the claim that failure could not be explained by intense disagreement over the policy objective (p. xx).

In figure 7, an example from Pressman and Wildavsky's (1983) examination of the EDA Oakland initiative is presented. The two actors are the EDA, the federal program sponsor, and World Airways, a local intermediary. To interpret implementation behavior from this perspective one must infer the preferences of participants over the possible outcomes. The preference orderings of the participants identify the nature of the strategic

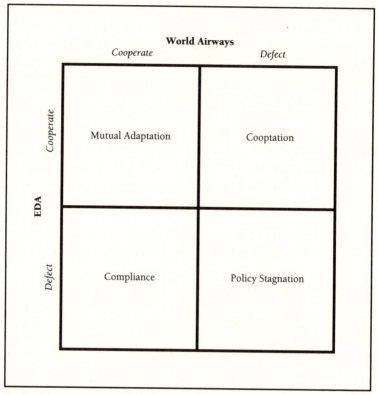

FIG. 7. World/EDA Game

interaction—mixed motive (one of several possible types), Deadlock, or Harmony.

If the interaction between the EDA and World Airways was a Prisoner's Dilemma, the most preferred outcome of the Oakland initiative for both participants would be unilateral defection. For World Airways, this would mean that EDA would fund the hangar construction project without the expectation of real changes in World's hiring practices. For EDA, it would mean achieving its minority employment goals without providing financial support to World Airways. Given their choice, it is plausible that each would express this preference. The second most preferred outcome would be mutual cooperation: World Airways would receive support for the hangar project in exchange for substantial efforts to recruit and hire minority workers targeted by EDA. The third most preferred outcome would be program stagnation—World would not change its employment practices and the EDA would not fund the hangar project. The least preferred outcome for each is exploitation at the hands of the other. For World Airways, this would mean making substantial changes in their hiring practices without receiving the expected financial assistance for the hangar project. For the EDA, this would mean providing financial assistance to complete the hangar project without achieving changes in minority employment.

The other possible interpretation is that interaction was Deadlock. In this context, exchange is not feasible because the costs of cooperation outweigh the benefits; policy design, not implementation, is the cause of failure. A crude comparison of benefits and costs could be asserted in which the value of the federal loans and grants to World Airways is insufficient compensation for the cost of federal intrusion into its personnel practices. Some evidence presented by Pressman and Wildavsky (1983) supports this interpretation (pp. 53–58).

Why, in the face of mutual interests, might participants in the Oakland initiative have failed to cooperate? The failure is not surprising because three characteristics that promote cooperation were absent from this case: (1) a history of interaction between the participants, (2) the expectation of future interaction, and (3) the commitment of dedicated resources to a program (Axelrod, 1984; Oye, 1985; Axelrod and Keohane, 1985). The absence of these factors suggests that interaction was unlikely to foster cooperation because the participants had not established a foundation for an ongoing relationship.

One factor that may have contributed to the difficulty in developing cooperation was the apparent decision to minimize the role of local business and civic leaders, substituting a direct sponsorship between the EDA and the Port of Oakland or selected private employers. Pressman and Wildavsky (1983) report that a "continuing disappointment to the EDA was its attempt to discover a decision making apparatus in Oakland that could throw its weight behind federal projects" (p. 51). In the absence of effective leadership from local institutions, the EDA decided to institute more direct action to assure that its employment objectives were achieved (pp. 25–26).

Evidence presented by Pressman and Wildavsky (1983) suggests that the concerns of the EDA were directed more toward community participation than toward established civic or business leadership. Initial contacts in Oakland bypassed city hall and focused upon community leadership (pp. 18–19); the eventual meeting with business leaders was organized by Mayor Houlihan with little participation from the EDA (p. 23); and the Employment Plan Review Board, the only local institutionalized participant in the Oakland initiative, was viewed by the EDA as a vehicle for community participation (pp. 26, 31). These decisions are likely to have aggravated rather than assuaged the concerns of employers about the implications of cooperation.

The authority paradigm would commend the decision to create direct sponsorship between commercial concerns and the EDA (excepting the participation of the Employment Plan Review Board) because it reduces the number of implementation participants. The exchange paradigm would concur, suggesting that it is wise to bypass Oakland's civic and business leaders because the initiative would be spared the buffeting created by the local political concerns of such participants.

Enhancing the role of Oakland's civic and business leaders would have meant that some revision of the initiative was likely. What gain from their participation could justify this? Officials concerned with local economic development are likely to have a history of interaction with employers in their jurisdiction. Their participation has value because it allows employers to develop expectations about the consequences of program participation. The history of cooperation toward development goals within the local community, in conjunction with the interest that local officials are likely to have exhibited in business performance, eases concern about the potential downside from a public-private venture. The EDA, lacking a track record, had an uncertain basis for soliciting cooperation and did not discover or create effective local institutions to do the job.

Other aspects of the program could have mitigated the lack of history that confronted the EDA in Oakland, but none are evident. There was no opportunity for reciprocity. An ongoing relationship makes cooperation more likely because organizations seek to establish and maintain responsible reputations with regular associates. This constrains behavior and reduces the fear of exploitation. But once the EDA had made its foray into Oakland, it was unlikely that other opportunities for interaction among the same participants would be created again. The reasonable expectation was that this was a one-shot deal and the uncertain urban agenda of the EDA (recall that this was an experimental initiative that involved the EDA in urban development problems for the first time) could only reinforce this perception.

Both parties were reluctant to commit themselves, each uncertain of the intentions of the other. The EDA made no investment to indicate good faith and commitment, keeping the option to defect open while demanding a commitment from World Airways (Pressman and Wildavsky, 1983, p. 44). World Airways sought to minimize its vulnerability by avoiding commitments and pledging only to "exert its best effort" to employ the EDA's target group (p. 57). The uncertainty created suspicion that manifested itself in the EDA's insistence upon a more strict employment contract as a condition for additional federal support and the reluctance of World to agree.

The regime framework would conclude that the failure of the EDA in Oakland was a consequence of the failure of policy formulators or implementation participants to create a context in which they could overcome their inclination not to cooperate. The lack of clear expectations about the implications of cooperation made all participants suspicious of the motives and intentions of others. In this atmosphere, each sought protection and avoided commitment. Such behavior can too easily be misinterpreted as confirmation of one's suspicion that the other participant is not trustworthy. As a result, mutual defection leads to policy stagnation.

Regime Development Beyond Oakland

A reasonable critic might suggest that the relevance of the regime framework is limited by its emphasis upon established relationships and expectations for the future. Granting that the "shadow of the future" is a powerful inducement for cooperation, the critic would observe that all policy initiatives cannot be implemented in ideal circumstances. In undertaking an experimental initiative, the national government may be reluctant (for good reasons) to make a perpetual commitment to the program. Beyond this, a common purpose of policy initiatives is to create new interorganizational relationships, not to build upon established ones. In these circumstances, does the regime framework offer constructive advice to policy formulators and implementation participants?

The regime literature contains several suggestions for policy formulators or implementation participants to improve the likelihood of cooperation and mutual adaptation. Robert Axelrod (1984, p. 133) suggests that an effective way to foster cooperation is to boost the reward that participants receive. Though this suggestion is most relevant to policy design, there are instances in which implementors too can restructure the payoffs received by participants. An example is found in Martha Derthick's report of the Fort Lincoln new town development in Washington, D.C. Implementors quieted local opposition to the project by offering to construct a new school in the affected neighborhood. As Derthick (1972) notes, "for the citizens' council to obstruct" the project "was to deprive the neighborhood of a benefit to which it attached a high value" (p. 33).

A second way to alter the expected payoffs of implementation participants is to create issue linkages; either "blackmail" or "backscratching" may be attempted (Axelrod and Keohane, 1985). The purpose of the linkage is to alter the anticipated payoff of a participant by joining the consequences of cooperation in one context to the interests of that party in another. A recent example of issue linkage was the threat of the federal government to withhold federal highway construction funds from states that refused to raise the minimum drinking age to twenty-one. As the example suggests, issue linkages are likely to be controversial and thus require action from policy formulators.

Cooperation also is more likely when grand programs are broken down into a series of smaller exchanges, reducing the gain from exploitation and the risk of cooperation (Axelrod, 1984; Oye, 1985). (A noteworthy aspect of the Oakland initiative is that the negotiations between the EDA and local employers were comprehensive.) Fostering cooperation may be an externality of the budget cycles that control funding for many public programs; this suggests that ongoing, institutionalized commitments are more likely to promote cooperation than occasional, lump-sum grants.

Implementation participants could foster cooperation by clarifying "standards of conduct" defining cooperative behavior (Oye, 1985). This strategy makes unintended defection less likely and clarifies the expectations of both parties. Some evidence of this exists in the Oakland case with the EDA's plan to negotiate employment contracts, though the employment contracts are not ideal examples. The EDA attempted to bind World Airways to specific employment commitments (Pressman and Wildavsky, 1983, p. 43), not so much defining cooperative behavior as assigning responsibility for program success. A more constructive strategy would have seen the EDA seeking "transparency" in World's employment processes (Oye, 1985). By defining procedures to share information, facilitating observation to assure cooperation, the EDA could have used the contract negotiations as a constructive tool for regime development.

COMPLEXITY AND
IMPLEMENTATION REGIMES

Complexity—indicated by numerous implementation participants and decision points (Pressman and Wildavsky, 1983)—

may affect the strategic relationship between participants, making it more difficult to identify and realize common interests (Oye, 1985). Complexity also may increase transaction and information costs, making regime maintenance more costly.

When implementation occurs in a context that is not adequately described by the two participant strategic interaction, the regime framework may be expanded to incorporate the special problems of multiple participants. Situations that involve multiple participants are more difficult to organize for the pursuit of common interest because transaction and information costs are increased. Two substantial changes are expected when implementation is complex (Oye, 1985). First, an elevation in the number of implementation participants increases the anonymity of each, inviting the possibility of undetected defection. If it is impossible to know in advance which implementation participants are likely to defect, information to monitor performance and identify defection must be gathered from the entire population of participants (or perhaps from a rotating sample). Information costs increase with each new participant and, given limits on the budget for information, so does the likelihood that defection is not detected. Second, sanction is less feasible with numerous participants, as the costs of sanction may not be imposed directly and exclusively upon the target. The burden of paperwork that often accompanies participation in federal programs is an apt example. The ostensible purpose of such periodic reporting is to encourage compliance with federal regulations and to detect violations of rule or procedure. However, the cost of compliance with these reporting requirements is not limited to those who have, or likely would have, violated federal guidelines; it is imposed upon all participants.

Although the regime framework recognizes that increases in the number of participants complicates the process of regime development and operation, in contrast to conventional wisdom, less is not always more. Additional participants may improve the possibilities for implementation success if they contribute to mechanisms that create trust and promote cooperation.

THE DYNAMICS OF REGIME CHANGE

One implication of the regime framework is that implementation regimes change as they operate. Over time, the operation of an implementation regime makes cooperation and policy coordination more likely. This may have important effects upon the strategic context in which implementation occurs. If so, the strategic context of the implementation process may change in accord with a predictable dynamic: a pattern of change emerges that reflects the history and character of interaction between implementation participants.

Regardless of its initial level of development, an implementation regime matures as a consequence of the interaction among implementation participants. As was noted earlier, a key element in inducing cooperation is the history of constructive interaction, which creates expectations about the consequences of cooperation. Implementation participants are more inclined to cooperate when they enjoy a history of interaction with other participants. Beyond this, the political context in which implementation participants operate changes in response to regime operation. As the regime operates and provides services, it develops a constituency that becomes a source of power and a constraint. The constituency can defend the program and claim resources but demands continued services in exchange.

The preceding discussion has treated strategic and institutional context as separate entities in regime development. However, there is a relationship between them that influences the likelihood of gaining cooperation from implementation participants. Aspects of the context in which implementation occurs may be related in two important ways. First, a history of cooperation and policy coordination is generated by the operation of the regime's institutions. This is a source of good will and convergent expectations that can reduce fear of exploitation by implementation participants. Second, the strategic context in which implementation occurs is redefined as implementation participants become part of an institutionalized service delivery mechanism that generates continuous demands from constituents and program sponsors. If this occurs, aspects of regime development are complementary, strengthening the regime directly—by making the institution more effective—and indirectly—by creating a more manageable strategic context.

The Improving Prospects for Cooperation

The dynamic of change in the implementation process is depicted in figure 8 as two trend lines: one, sloping downward, indicates the cost/risk of cooperation, and the other, sloping upward, indicates the cost/risk of defection. (Note that these are trend lines and hence are not assumed to seek an equilibrium point.) The upward slope in the cost/risk of defection suggests that defection is most attractive in the initial stages of the implementation process. At this time, defection is a more viable option because the program has yet to create a cohesive group of constituents to demand continued services. What pressure may exist is for new benefits, not protection from loss. As time passes, the cost/risk of defection (and the possibility of policy stagnation that it raises) increases.

These changes occur because services provided by the implementation process have nurtured a constituency that demands continued satisfaction. Select policy formulators, implementation participants, clients, and advocacy groups make up the constituency. Eventually, implementation participants come to view continuation of the program as an important task, both in terms of providing valued public services and bureaucratic survival.

The opposite is true of the cost/risk of cooperation. In the earliest stages of the implementation process, the cost/risk of cooperation is highest. To appear too accommodating early in the process may increase costs because it invites more aggressive behavior from other implementation participants. Beyond this, the risk of cooperation decreases over time as the history of interaction creates mutual expectations that make behavior predictable and reduces the perceived risk of exploitation. Familiarity also breeds trust.

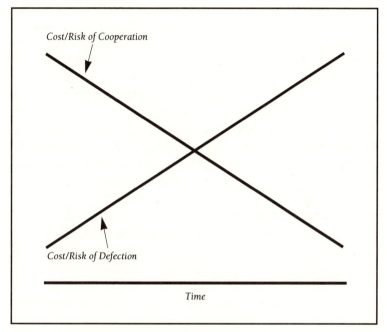

FIG. 8. Dynamics of Regime Change Over Time

To understand how the implementation problem changes over time in this context, examine the trend lines together, focusing upon the gaps between them. In the initial periods, implementation is most difficult since the likelihood of defection—and consequently stagnation from mutual defection—is greatest. However, over time, this tendency is self-correcting. The tables will turn; the trends won't stop at the intersection point. The likelihood of cooperation increases later so that cooperation and mutual adaptation become more likely.

The Role of Professionalism

Some evidence to complement this claim is found in Peterson, Rabe, and Wong, *When Federalism Works* (1986). In their discussion of the implementation of redistributive programs—

a rough analog to a mixed motive strategic context—the authors suggest that federal programs can require a long time to operate effectively (p. 158). This time is required because policy professionals must "develop" legitimacy and commitment to federal program objectives (pp. 161–62). Once this development occurs, these professionals become committed to the pursuit of federal goals and tend to identify more with the program than the city in which they live (pp. 190–91). If such programs can be implemented within established organizations controlled by professionals and guided by professional norms, federal programs are more likely to be successfully implemented (p. 189). Such professionalized programs are more likely to survive and prosper because their mission is clear, they are effectively managed, and they enjoy client support (p. 228).

The Changing Strategic Context

How do changes in institutional context affect the strategic context in which implementation occurs? As changes occur in institutional context over time, a new type of strategic context can emerge. Even when the implementation process is initiated in the most pessimistic possible mixed motive context—Prisoner's Dilemma—over time, the strategic context will change to make cooperation more likely. Over time, the CC point (mutual accommodation) will migrate to the northeast and the DD point (policy stagnation) will migrate to the southwest. These changes, associated in previous discussions with the comparison of Prisoner's Dilemma, Stag Hunt, and Chicken, can create a context in which the problems of inducing cooperation are substantially reduced.

POLICY REFORM

If the problems of gaining cooperation from reluctant partners are reduced over time, a strategy for implementing federal programs based upon program reform is implied. If the implementation problem becomes less serious over time, the initial periods following program development are those in which the program is most vulnerable to stagnation or exploitation from reluctant partners and federal program sponsors. During this period, implementation and commitment to program objectives can be developed by emphasizing the distributive aspects of the program. More emphasis should be placed upon providing federal resources and accommodating state or local needs flexibly while soliciting the cooperation of reluctant partners.

Over time, program reforms can be introduced, indicating shifts in federal priorities. When this happens, an implicit issue linkage is created. The interest that reluctant partners have in continuing to enjoy the initial, more distributive federal program is linked to new federal demands. If the regime framework and the observations of Peterson, Rabe, and Wong (1986) are correct, a context for implementing reform will often be one in which federal demands are well received by a committed professional program staff.

The Reform Dilemma

This is encouraging news that suggests that only a lack of patience prevents constructive government policy. However, a dilemma exists. Reform of the program may require a substantial catalyst, usually reformulation of the program by policy formulators, because the patterns of interaction that are institutionalized in the regime are not easily disrupted. The same constituent groups that make defection less attractive to implementation participants also make it more difficult to substantially alter the program.[7] The objections of constituent groups may prevent policy formulators from mustering the required political will. Those reform initiatives that are successful are likely to be distributive, adding new classes of beneficiaries or levels of benefits without disturbing the benefits enjoyed by current constituents. The apparent dilemma is that as reform becomes more feasible in the implementation process it becomes less feasible from the perspective of policy formulators.

One escape from the dilemma may be found in detailed policy formulation. The extent to which the regime is developed
defines the difficulty of the implementation problem. A highly
developed implementation regime is one in which the cost/risk
of cooperation is low relative to the cost/risk of defection. If the
initial policy formulation process can craft a highly developed
regime, more ambitious program requirements can be incorporated into the initial program design. This would avoid the
necessity of later reformulating the initiative and escape the
dilemma.

If these changes in strategic context occur over time, one
should have modest expectations for implementation performance in the time that closely follows the development of a
policy program. However, as the implementation regime more
fully develops, it is possible to implement reforms to the program that might not have been successfully implemented when
the regime was less mature. This would suggest that a longitudinal research design that focuses upon policy reform and its
relationship to measures of program performance would be
most appropriate to examine the implications of the regime
framework. Aside from its advantages as a research tool (see
Krist and Jung, 1982), the longitudinal approach also is most
appropriate given the dynamic evolution of the regime posited
by the framework.

CONCLUSION

The implementation regime framework implies that the strategic context in which implementation occurs has an important
influence on the likelihood of cooperation. However, the possibilities to induce cooperation are not limited to manipulation
of strategic context. Aspects of institutional design and unilateral actions may be undertaken to make the strategic problems
inherent in mixed motive interactions more likely to induce
cooperation.

But inducing cooperation is not an activity that occurs in a political vacuum. To the contrary, the political consequences of protecting and promoting different values in public decision making are likely to be significant. In the following chapter, the political consequences of regime design decisions are described.

4   THE POLITICS OF
        IMPLEMENTATION REGIMES

THE IMPLEMENTATION of national policy in a liberal, federal polity plays out an essential dynamic—the resolution of tension between centralized and diffuse authority. Constitutional principles that demand diffuse authority place national policy initiatives in a tense environment; implementation participants must reconcile the centralizing forces inherent in the formulation of national policy initiatives with the existing diffusion of authority and control of policy resources. The resolution of this tension falls to implementation regimes.

Implementation regimes meld the means and ends of the policy-making process; the structures and processes of regimes represent values important to public decision making and means to promote those values. Though it takes many forms, the essential value conflict in a liberal, federal polity is between central and diffuse authority. How the regime structures and reconciles competition between these values may have important political consequences.

If it is not possible to determine implementation outcomes in advance (following critiques of the authority paradigm—limits of rationality, the inefficacy of authority, and respect for constitutional principles that value diffuse authority), policy must evolve as it moves through the implementation process. This evolution, though not completely predictable in its effect upon the outcome, can be expected to reflect the interests and priorities of those positioned to express their desires. Implicitly or explicitly, implementation regimes accommodate some values, making them central to the evolution of public policy, and discount others. Who is empowered by regime formulation? What are the consequences of regime design decisions for the evolution of policy?

POWER IN THE IMPLEMENTATION PROCESS

Harold Seidman (1976) equates power with position in the policy making process. This implies that who is positioned to influence policy is a matter of crucial concern because the creation of partnerships to implement national policy empowers a select few who are given the ability to interpret and improve (influence) policy. In this way, position is a source of power.

The creation of partnerships generates power and the ability to govern in a context of diffuse authority (see chapter 2 for discussion). But, in the implementation process, power is a paradox. The power generated by partnership is also a constraint—it creates the ability to do some, but not all, things (Stone, 1989). Partnerships empower the federal government and implementation participants but establish a limited competency—an ability to accomplish policy objectives that, inevitably, reflect the capacity, concerns, and perceptions of selected implementation participants. In this way, the power generated by partnership creates possibilities and limits.

Attractive Partners

If implementation participants influence the evolution of policy, what would make commercial firms or state and local governments attractive partners in federal policy? These institutions are formidable adversaries. Why not avoid them and seek cooperation from others less able to challenge federal priorities and objectives?

One answer is politics. National policy formulators, especially members of Congress, are subjected to crosscutting pressures that create concern both for national effectiveness and protection of key local constituencies. It may be that the structure of national representation creates a context for national decision making in which political considerations—albeit legitimate ones—serve to systematically challenge leadership by the federal government. And this disability is not limited even by the exclusive powers provided to the federal government under the constitution. (As was noted earlier, Elazar [1972] has found that federal policy design typically exceeds constitutional requirements for state and local involvement.) Are political considerations the only rationale? Is it inevitable that political considerations are at odds with the creation of effective partnerships to implement national policy?

Clarence Stone (1989) has offered an alternate rationale— that there is a tendency for policy makers to seek partnerships with those who control "enough resources to have leverage in an otherwise gridlocked world" (p. 230). The most attractive partners are those "who are organized, who control essential resources, and who have the capacity to engage in a dependable system of cooperation." He suggests that what is at issue is not the domination of one group over another, but the creation of a "capacity to act and accomplish goals" (p. 229). From this perspective, federal policy makers may be inclined to include firms or state and local governments in federal programs because the information, resources, and authority of these rivals is vital to generating the capacity to accomplish national policy goals. More formidable adversaries are also more attractive partners. If so, power is a source of position.

Political Consequences

If both Stone and Seidman are correct, important political consequences follow. Control of resources makes some elements of society more attractive as partners in the implementation process. This partnership potential empowers them, enhancing their ability to influence federal policy in two ways. First, influence will be exhibited in policy design, as pains are taken to develop policy that is likely to accommodate the interests of those who control key resources. Second, as implementation proceeds, the participation of these partners causes policy to evolve in a manner that reflects their priorities and concerns. By promoting select options and making others infeasible, those who control resources desired by the federal government enjoy unusual influence over the scope and content of federal policy. This suggests that federal policy is likely to have a strong status quo orientation—reflecting the existing distribution of resources—that protects the most powerful, established institutions of society.

In this way, position and power are complementary. Position is a source of power; but power is also a source of position. Those who are well positioned in the implementation process are empowered. However, those who are selected to be well positioned are likely to be those who are powerful. The selection of implementation participants reflects the deliberate choice of policy formulators but also affirms the existing capacity of social institutions.

As some are empowered by position, implicit political judgments are made in the implementation process. If so, the design of regimes and the evolution of policy within them is a political process. Consideration of the regime framework is incomplete unless the political consequences of regime development are noted.

A REGIME TYPOLOGY

In this chapter, eight ideal types of implementation regimes are identified through the development of a two-dimensional classification scheme. Each type of regime represents a different sort of political arrangement with implications for representation of interest and for the generation of public effectiveness.

The regime typology is created by the cross-classification of two continuums: the distribution of public authority and the action sector. The continuum describing the distribution of public authority has poles that are labeled *centralized* and *diffuse*. To clarify the meaning of this dimension, the continuum could be divided into three ideal categories. When authority is centralized (note the discussion in chapter 2 of the difficulty of achieving this in practice), the federal government acts alone to implement policy. At the opposite pole, where authority is diffuse, public authority is held by many, even those outside the formal organs of government (this should not imply that it is equally or "equitably" distributed). Between these extremes is the realm of shared authority. In this context, public authority is contained within many different formal organizations of government (for example, federal, state, or local).

The second continuum is the action sector with poles labeled *government* and *market*. Though all national policy initiatives imply action by federal policy formulators, there is variation in the extent to which action to implement policy is taken directly by government or indirectly through market mechanisms. When government is the action sector, interaction occurs between federal employees and citizens as clients or targets of policy. When the market is the action sector, government acts to establish a pseudomarket that affects clients or targets indirectly by providing access or means to participate in market transactions. Between these extremes is the realm of joint action in which government and market forces interact to implement policy.

The implementation regime typology is created when these two dimensions are combined (see figure 9). The horizontal dimension represents the distribution of public authority. The vertical dimension indicates the action sector. Nine categories, but only eight types of implementation regimes, are created by the intersection of these two dimensions. At the top extreme left is the bureaucratic regime—the organizational ideal for the au-

Action Sector \ Distribution of Public Authority	*Centralized*	*Shared*	*Diffuse*
Government	Bureaucratic	Federalist	Pluralist
Joint	Federal Regulatory	Shared Regulatory	Corporate
Market	Federal Quasi market	Shared Quasi market	Market*

FIG. 9. Implementation Regime Typology. Market* is not considered an implementation regime.

thority paradigm. This type of regime features centralized public authority and action taken directly by government. The spontaneous order of the market is at the bottom extreme right. The market is the organizational ideal of the exchange paradigm but is excluded from the list of implementation regimes because it is not goal oriented (for clarification of this point, see the discussion of spontaneous order in chapter 2 and the origins of implementation regimes in chapter 3).

Aside from these familiar extremes, seven other implementation regime types are identified. Within the governmental action sector, shared authority creates a federalist regime, and diffuse authority produces a pluralist regime. Within the joint action sector, centralized authority creates federal regulatory regimes, shared authority produces shared regulatory regimes, and diffuse authority creates corporate regimes. Within the market action sector, centralized authority creates federal quasi markets and shared authority creates shared quasi markets.

It is important to note that the diffuse pole of public authority should not imply that the distribution of influence over public decisions is natural, desirable, or equitable. To the contrary, regimes of the pluralist and corporate types often are means to achieve political ends that affect the ability of groups to influence policy, regardless of the ethical or political implications of such influence. It should also be noted that the regime types are not mutually exclusive; some of the characteristics of different regime types are shared, but each has a distinct characteristic that sets it apart from the others. Each of these ideal regime types are manifestations of the essential value conflict that must be resolved in governing a liberal, federal polity: the resolution of tension between centralization of authority to make policy coherent, consistent, and goal oriented and the desire for diffuse authority to promote liberty and make policy more robust and efficient. While each regime type represents one way to implement policy, and hence one way to deal with the inherent tension between central and diffuse authority, the categories are quite broad and within each several subtypes may exist. In the following sections, the eight types of implementation regimes are described and illustrated.

BUREAUCRATIC REGIME

The most centralized of all regimes is the bureaucratic regime. This type of regime seeks to consolidate public authority into a single, central governmental authority to direct policy. A bureaucratic regime attempts to impose terms of cooperation on other elements of society through the operation of a bureaucratic control system consisting of three elements: (1) rules to direct the behavior of subordinates, (2) penalties for noncompliance, and (3) enforcement mechanisms. Typically, a bureaucratic regime will arrange periodic reporting of information to monitor those subject to its authority and attempt to control their behavior with penalties for noncompliance.

In the ideal, a bureaucratic regime values knowledge, technical expertise, and administrative efficiency. However, the term *efficiency* can mean many things in this context and may be used to justify standard procedures and performance that seem to belie the meaning of the term. Consistent marks of bureaucratic efficiency are routinization of problems and solutions, the tendency to reduce costs to the organization by managing the provision of services on its terms rather than the preferences of its clients, and the inclination to externalize costs by requiring extensive effort from the clients to receive services (examples might include numerous forms to complete and long lines for service).

When a bureaucratic regime implements policy, an implicit assertion is made that a "technical" solution to a problem can be identified, though it may still be in the early stages of development. Thus, politics is regarded as interference with the execution of the "proper" solution to the problem. Of course, the creation of such a regime may be instead an attempt to impose a particular solution by empowering those who support it; rather than being apolitical, the bureaucratic regime may simply exhibit a political outlook that is less flexible and participatory than others.

The conflict central to this sort of regime is conflict between bureaucratic authority and individual liberty. There is always tension between the bureau's need for information and use of sanctions to induce compliance and the privacy and autonomy of the individual. The Internal Revenue Service (IRS) is an example of a bureaucratic regime that commonly exhibits such tension. Its use of information and penalties to manipulate its clients, its perverse "efficiency," and its complexity make the IRS a classic example of the bureaucratic regime.

Death and Taxes

Will Rogers used to say: "The Income Tax has made more Liars out of the American people than golf has." But, by many measures, U.S. citizens exhibit a remarkable tendency to co-operate with the federal government in its administration of the Personal Income Tax. Authority for the federal government to collect income taxes is derived from the sixteenth amendment (1913) to the Constitution of the United States: "The Congress shall have the power to lay and collect taxes on incomes, from whatever source derived, without apportionment among the several States, and without regard to any census or enumeration."

Many different explanations could be advanced to account for the tendency of U.S. citizens to pay their taxes: it could be a result of the public spiritedness of our citizens; it could be a rational calculation of taxpayers in response to the penalty that the IRS may exact from those who do not comply. However, some might claim not to understand our inclination to pay taxes at all.

Individual taxpayers should not be naturally inclined to "co-operate" with the IRS in its mission to collect taxes. Mancur Olson (1971) argues that it is in each individual's interest to "free ride," to avoid taxes while all others pay theirs. To anyone who has paid taxes, Olson's argument must ring true. It would be difficult to imagine a context in which the conflict of interest between an agent of government and the individual citizen was more intense.

Given this, how and why do we pay taxes? Part of the answer may be found in coercive authority—criminal penalties for non-compliance with tax law. However, this explanation is incomplete. Any realistic assessment of tax compliance in the United States would note that tax compliance is not homogeneous—tax compliance is probably lower in the "cash economy."[1]

Tax Compliance in the Cash Economy

Betty is one of the working poor. A sixty-two-year-old widow who has recently taken the early retirement option under provisions of OASDI of the social security system, she has, for the past several years, supported herself and her aged mother (who also receives a modest social security benefit) on payments received from a relative in exchange for child care services. The

$150 per week, when combined with social security payments, is sufficient to provide the approximately $1000 per month the household requires—that is as long as no income or FICA taxes are paid. Although her tax bill would be modest, none of the income earned from providing child care (approximately $30,000 over the past four years) has been reported to the IRS. Each year when Betty files her tax return she risks the wrath of the federal government. Why?

Betty is not unusually dishonest, but she enjoys an edge that many U.S. citizens would likely exploit in similar circumstances. Without a substantial paper trail to implicate her, the IRS is unlikely to discover her noncompliance and enforce its penalties. Cash payments from a relative are difficult to trace; this undermines the effectiveness of the IRS at gaining cooperation from taxpayers like Betty.

Considered more carefully, the real cooperation in administering the income tax system comes not from individual taxpayers, but from private sector intermediaries who provide the information that compels individuals to account for income earned (the familiar W2 and W4 forms). Lacking this sort of information, the IRS must find alternate forms of income estimation (as it did for those employees of restaurants whose primary income is from tips) or accept the limited capacity of its system. To reduce tax fraud in child care services the IRS now requires that payments made for child care that are claimed as a tax deduction include forms that provide information about the individual paid to perform the service.

The legal obligation to pay one's taxes is supported by a system of carefully constructed information flows from a diverse group of intermediaries (most often commercial enterprises). The system of organization—rules, sanctions, and information—induces cooperation from individuals by making noncompliance easier to detect. More important than the incentive structure—penalties for noncompliance apply in both cash and noncash economies—is the transparency of the earned income situation of taxpayers whose employers send required paperwork in to the IRS.

It may seem strange that private sector intermediaries could be made such dependable partners in a costly, complex administrative scheme in which interests are so clearly in conflict. But consider the position of the employer. If he fails to file the proper forms, the employee may provide information that would indicate his noncompliance to the IRS. If he does comply, he enjoys documented expenses that reduce the tax liability of his business. But what keeps the employer from exploiting this opportunity—overestimating the employee's income to enhance his own tax benefit—by frustrating the system with inaccurate information about the employee's wages? Copies of the information are distributed to every participant in the process. This simple administrative tool amounts to a system of impressive, but limited, effectiveness.

It is an adage among taxpayers that the IRS has its way on income so the only way to tip the balance is on interpretation of deductions. The system limits the ability of taxpayers to reduce their tax liability by failing to report earned income, and this affects the likely character of tax cheating. Outside the cash economy, tax cheating is much more likely to take the form of exaggerated deductions than unreported income.

The administrative system that supports tax compliance is a bureaucratic regime of limited scope and effectiveness. In the cash economy, the IRS is much less effective at gaining cooperation, not because people are any less inclined to cooperate, nor because legal obligations are any less binding, nor because the penalties for noncompliance are any less severe; but because the system of administration does not exist to reliably report earned income. Recent policy changes, for example bank withholding of interest earned or estimates of cash gratuities provided to restaurant workers, can be seen as attempts by the IRS to overcome deficiencies in its information flow to expand the scope of its bureaucratic regime.

FEDERALIST REGIMES

A federalist regime reflects the tension inherent in the conflict between centralized and diffuse authority; it is shaped by the desire to have effective national leadership within a system of constituent states that creates a diffusion of political authority. The federalist regime is distinctive in three ways: first, the federal government remains an active implementation participant in federalist regimes (as opposed to the passive participation of federal courts that may enforce rights or obligations). Second, the basis for distributing political authority and other resources are the territories that constitute the constituent states of the republic. Third, there are constitutional considerations that limit the consolidation of authority within the federal government.

The problem for federal policy formulators is to induce cooperation from state or local governments in support of national policy goals. There are many different ways in which federal arrangements may be structured so as to induce cooperation. Among the most important aspects of design for federalist regimes are: (1) the conditions for participation in federal programs; (2) the rationing system applied to distribute federal resources; (3) federal programmatic requirements and constraints; and (4) the distribution of costs. When designing a federalist regime to induce cooperation, key issues include: whether the relationship is durable and ongoing (reflecting the existence of a shadow of the future); whether federal funds are discretionary (indicating more possibility to influence the purposes of federal policy); and who foots the bill (indicating the nature of financial incentives). The dimensions of the federalist regime design are summarized in figure 10.

Grants in Aid

Programmatic constraints, or the extent to which flexibility exists in the objectives or contents of a program, are one key aspect of the federalist regime design. Programmatic constraints exist on three levels: formula grants, block grants, and categorical grants. Formula grants, the least flexible, are tied to the provision of specific services designed to achieve federal program objectives. Block grants, whose mandates and requirements are open to broad interpretation at the state or local level, are the

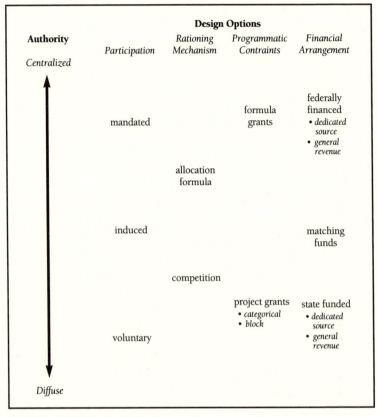

FIG. 10. Federalist Regime Design

most flexible. Categorical grants assume the middle ground in which the purposes of federal policy are outlined, but the specific means to achieve policy objectives are not.

Block grants tend to reinforce the established political order. The ability of a state or locality to direct federal aid to its own priorities allows well-positioned participants to make decisions that reflect their priorities. The practical consequence of this is that favored state and local constituencies will receive the lion's share of the federal assistance. This process may occur subtly as state or local leaders, who are positioned to define the interests and priorities of their jurisdiction, influence the direction of federal policy with little opposition. The lack of opposition may reflect organizational arrangements that limit public participation and disarm critics or might reveal the political flexibility that may come from spending money that is not generated by local sources (Stoker, 1987).

Categorical grants are more likely to challenge the established distribution of power. Of course, that is sometimes a stated or implicit purpose of this sort of federal initiative. Categorical grants may bypass established political powers to motivate coalitions of support within a state or locality. The ability of these coalitions to press their demands at the state or local level is enhanced by the promise that the federal government is going to pay a portion of the cost. Coalitions that are too weak in the absence of federal support are empowered by the federal program. The opportunity to gain federal benefits congeals the coalition of support and places the issue on the state's policy agenda. To avoid the charge that they have missed an opportunity to bring home the bacon, state and local officials are often inclined to be responsive and advance the coalition's agenda.

Competitive Federalist Regimes

Competition is a rationing mechanism used when policy that enjoys broad support at all levels of government is available in limited supply. Usually, competition occurs for program inputs (dollars, authority, or manpower) within a framework developed by federal program sponsors. The competition may occur within the context of federalism—states may compete for scarce resources—or within the context of a market—in which firms or private entities are the competitors. Although entry into the competition is voluntary, this does not imply an absence of conflict. In a competitive context, the central conflict is between those who wish to enjoy the resources without obligation and those who seek to use the resources to induce changes in behavior from those who receive the award.

A key aspect of the competitive federalist regime is that the federal program sponsor has an exit option—the option not to participate. This is a rare feature among federal policy initiatives. The usual practice is for the federal government to commit itself to participation in some public program and seek to induce others to join. For this reason, the competitive regime is thought to substantially enhance the power of the federal program sponsor.

The enhanced power of the federal program sponsor is most evident in the initial stages of the process. At that time, the solicitous attitude of possible recipients makes them seem ready to do almost anything to receive the federal grant. However, this advantage may be fleeting. Two aspects of the competitive regime are responsible for this. One is the natural development of the program over time. If the federal government becomes committed to the program, withdrawal becomes painful and embarrassing, limiting the viability of the exit option. Second, the "one shot" nature of the program makes it difficult to create a substantial shadow for the future. This implies that a state or local agency or commercial firm may have little incentive to follow up with commitments made at the proposal stage when actual program operation begins. It is more likely that quiet but significant changes in the purposes of the program, or attempts to renegotiate program requirements (always explained as a response to unforeseen circumstances), will follow the award.

Examples of Federalist Regimes

An extensive illustration of the federalist regime type has been presented in the first chapter's discussion of the Fort Lincoln new town initiative. That program was implemented through a voluntary, competitive, categorical grant and loan program, financed by federal funds. Aid to Families with Dependent Children is a second example. This program is implemented through mandatory, formula-based allocations of grants financed by federal, state, and local governments.

PLURALIST REGIMES

The pluralist regime is unique among the forms discussed here because rather than reflecting and reinforcing the status quo, it is created for the purpose of moving the existing distribution of power to a new equilibrium. This is done by empowering new actors or groups in a context in which all participants bargain for advantage and influence over policy. A key feature of pluralist policy initiatives is that interest groups are given the benefit of political legitimacy for their claims against other societal institutions.

Pluralist policy initiatives are often declarations of rights to classes of individuals without clear administrative means to enforce those rights. A common practice for the federal government is to define some sort of group right, recognizing and rewarding existing groups or providing a visible policy stake around which groups are likely to form. In this way, the development of pluralist policy sometimes stands as a counterexample to the usual pluralist assumption that groups have interests that they organize to pursue in the public arena. By creating opportunities for individuals or groups to affect policy, pluralist initiatives can create or congeal interests, reversing the causal arrow of pluralism (Walker, 1983).

The pluralist regime is characterized by unstructured competition between groups for control of policy (unstructured in the sense that the competition is not directed into specific administrative channels). Often competition to influence policy occurs outside institutions that are the nominal homes of "policy formulators" and on a schedule that reflects the personal agenda of participants rather than the imperatives of the policy-making process.

The effectiveness of participants in a pluralist regime is in part a reflection of their vitality, cohesion, and access to disposable resources. Unlike the federalist regime, effectiveness does not come from an established position in the policy-making process nor from a reliable source of public resources; rather, effectiveness results from an assertion of rights and interests in many settings. As a result, the court system is a common home for the resolution of conflict in pluralist regimes, reflecting both the passive nature of pluralist policy and the tendency for pluralist initiatives to be defined in terms of legal "rights." Federal policy for education of handicapped children is an example of the pluralist regime.

Handicapped Education

The 1975 Education for All Handicapped Children Act guaranteed an appropriate public education (at public expense) for all children, regardless of disability. The act is a federal law which requires local schools to provide education services for students within their jurisdiction. However, the act did not provide guidelines for what sorts of services were appropriate, nor did it provide the means through which such services were to be delivered or financed.

The force of the act was to create (or affirm) a legal right to a free public education for handicapped students—a population historically underserved by the public education system. The small number of such students made them politically impotent in local education funding decisions. The law had the purpose and effect of tipping the balance away from local school administrators and elected officials and toward handicapped advocates, handicapped students, and their parents. These empowered groups could use the federal mandate to negotiate settlements with local officials or to seek relief in federal court.

Absent federal standards for appropriate services in this area, local variation is likely to exist both in the nature of the demands that confront school administrators and the solutions that are enacted. This reflects the importance of the capability of the individual or group to motivate change within the pluralist regime.

REGULATORY REGIMES

The implementation regime typology contains two types of regulatory regimes: federal and shared. In a federal regulatory regime, regulation is conducted by federal agencies according to national standards. In shared regulatory regimes, more state or local variation exists in the establishment of standards and enforcement practices. To clarify the sources of variation possible under shared regulation, it should be noted that regulatory goals, even if quite specific, may have little teeth without enforcement procedures to back them up. Thus, two states or localities that have similar regulatory standards may differ in their enforcement vigor. Strong standards with lax enforcement can thus be a form of symbolic compliance that creates the appearance, but not the reality, of regulatory authority.

Incentives for states and localities, which must compete for investment by attracting and retaining industry, are thought to inhibit vigorous enforcement of stringent regulatory standards (see Dresang and Gosling, 1989). However, in some states, examples of rigorous standards and enforcement procedures also can be found (for example, California's stricter emissions standards for automobiles).

A regulatory regime is distinct because of its limited scope. A limited intervention into the market seeks to enjoy the benefits of liberal economic organization without permitting commercial concerns to be completely independent of political authority. (This view is consistent with Michael Reagan's [1987] view of regulation as "the halfway house of American political economy.") The central conflict in regulatory regimes is in the contrary desires of federal policy formulators to constrain and direct the behavior of firms while retaining a market economy. One desire pulls toward centralized authority, the other toward authority that is diffuse.[2]

A key issue in the design of regulatory regimes is whether the regulated party must implement a standardized solution. Regulation may be conducted in such a manner that a specific solution to the problem is imposed upon the regulated party. If so, the regulatory authority provides a standard "solution" to the problem that is thought to be appropriate in all situations.[3] The key regulatory problem in this context is to identify the parties who are required to implement the solution and to gather information (from direct observation or data provided by the regulated party) to assure compliance.

Alternately, regulation may be conducted so that goals or objectives are provided, but the regulated party is free to determine how best to meet regulatory requirements. In this circumstance, there can be more variation in the nature of solutions. This complicates the regulatory problem because it is now necessary to affirm that the solution works. This requires the development of testing facilities or on-site inspection for gathering information or the provision of test data from the regulated party. Of course information provided by the regulated parties may be subject to strategic manipulation. (Such manipulation was revealed in recent controversies dealing with the certification of generic drugs by the Food and Drug Administration.)

FEDERAL REGULATORY REGIMES: AUTOMOBILE FUEL ECONOMY

The Department of Transportation (DOT) has authority to regulate the fuel economy of automobiles from the Energy Policy and Conservation Act (EPCA) of 1975. Under the auspices of the EPCA, the DOT administers corporate average fuel economy (CAFE) compliance based upon a calculation of fuel economy performance conducted by the Environmental Protection Agency (EPA). In a reversal of policy under the administration of President Reagan, new and more demanding standards for automobile fuel economy have been promulgated. The reversal came as no surprise, given the dramatic rise in gasoline prices early in 1989 and the concern expressed by the Bush administration about environmental damages due to oil spills and the greenhouse effect.

The regulatory procedure estimates, through test procedures originally designed to gauge automobile emissions performance, the fuel economy of each model in simulated city and highway driving. Average performance for each model is calculated based upon a weighted average of the fuel economy achieved in the two simulations. This figure, the fuel economy of a given model, is combined with other models to calculate an average that accounts for the proportion of a manufacturer's production that each model represents. Failure to meet the CAFE standard is punishable by fines that amount to $10 per .1 mpg violation per unit; an amount which can be substantial because the fine is levied upon each and every unit produced by the manufacturer. From production figures supplied by the manufacturer, regulators calculate the fleet average for the mix of cars produced and levy fines where appropriate.

The CAFE standard was a target for regulatory reform during the Reagan presidency. The President's Commission on Regulatory Relief recommended abandoning the standard, a position echoed by then Secretary of DOT James Burnley IV, who reduced CAFE standards to 26.5 mpg for 1989 models. President Bush's secretary of DOT, Samuel Skinner, raised the standard to 27.5 mpg for 1990 models.

Strategic Behavior During Implementation

Continuing implementation problems have occurred as a consequence of the strategic response of automobile manufacturers to the regulatory procedures. In a report to the Congress that focused upon the EPA testing procedures, many of these problems were detailed (see "Automobile Fuel Economy"). Manufacturers could prepare model prototypes to perform especially well in EPA tests. This is done by engineering the prototype provided to the EPA to standards that will not exist in manufacturing or by altering the performance of the vehicle specifically for the test environment.

An important distinction in the regulations is between "domestic" and "imported" fleets. This provision, reflecting legislative intent, may have been intended to prevent circumvention of the regulations by bringing fuel-efficient imported autos into the United States and selling them under domestic nameplates. An obvious concern among legislators was the effect of CAFE standards upon employment in the automobile industry. The

regulations are intended to make domestically produced automobiles more fuel efficient; or, more precisely, to proscribe the
option of mixing inefficient domestic automobiles with fuel-
efficient imported ones to satisfy CAFE standards. The irony of
this case is that this attempt to limit the strategic options for
automobile manufacturers has created an opportunity to circumvent the regulations.

Ford Motor Company as Reluctant Partner

The response of the Ford Motor Company to the newly announced standard was to declare its intention to alter the mixture of components on some of its automobiles to change their
status from domestic to imported and vice versa. Ford's ability
to do this is a result of the scope and content of federal legislation, specifically the definition of "domestic" automobiles and
the desire of political leaders to protect the integrity of business.

The growth of the global economy has contributed to the
demise of traditional definitions of the source of automobiles.
"Domestic" automobiles may include many foreign-made components and even can be assembled outside the United States.
The government's definition of *domestic* is based upon the
"value added" at the domestic assembly sight. Beyond this, the
definition of a domestic automobile includes those assembled
in Canada.

One automobile produced by Ford that has relatively poor
fuel economy is the LTD Crown Victoria. Ford may shift this
automobile from the domestic class (that which figures into its
domestic average fuel economy standard) to the imported class
by changing the mixture of components that are acquired from
and added by domestic and imported sources. In addition, one
of Ford's more economical imported models, the Probe, could
become a domestic automobile, contributing a substantial improvement to the domestic fleet's fuel economy. The upshot is
that Ford may technically comply with—some would say circumvent—the regulation by altering the classification of some
automobiles, without improving their fuel efficiency.

SHARED REGULATORY REGIMES

The nature of regulatory regimes in which the federal government shares authority with state or local policy makers varies greatly. Michael Reagan (1987) has defined two primary types of regulation in which states participate as active partners: partial preemption and reverse-twist. He asserts that the more common type of regulation is partial preemption, in which the federal government creates statutory authority in a certain area but gives some of this authority back to the states. (State participation may be compulsory or voluntary). Less common is the reverse-twist regulatory initiative in which the states are able to delay or even veto policy decisions made at the federal level (the Nuclear Waste Policy Act of 1982 is an example of this type).

The Clean Air Act

An illustration of a joint regulatory program implemented by federal, state, and local policy makers is the Clean Air Act. Dresang and Gosling (1989) report that the act requires states to submit to federal regulators their own regulations that must meet minimum standards—participation is not voluntary, nor can states veto minimum federal standards. By Reagan's (1987) classification scheme, the Clean Air Act is a compulsory, partial preemption regulatory program.

Near the elementary school in Rothschild, Wisconsin, sits the Weyerhauser Paper Company, the town's largest employer.[4] Many students, especially those with asthmatic conditions, have been sickened while playing on the school's grounds when sulfur dioxide is released from the plant as a by-product of its production of pulp paper. The Clean Air Act of 1970 established the Environmental Protection Agency (EPA) as the federal authority regulating the discharge of various pollutants into the atmosphere and water. This authority was little comfort to students.

Weyerhauser fully complies with federal standards contained in EPA regulations. The EPA has adopted regulations that establish acceptable average levels of concentration of sulfur dioxide for three-hour time intervals. Within that three-hour time, concentrations may exceed EPA standards, so long as the three-hour average is met. Apparently, students who were outside during times when gas was released from the plant were exposed to levels of concentration that exceeded (for a short time period) acceptable health standards, causing some of them to become sick. However, because the plant's emissions were in compliance with the EPA's time-based averages, no action was taken by federal authorities to curtail the emissions.

The importance of shared authority is evident here from the refusal of the EPA to institute more stringent, national standards that would have accounted for short-term concentrations of the sickening gas. Local school officials, in concert with environmental activists and regional officials of the EPA, discovered and applied a little used state law to prevent pollution that causes a public health hazard. When charged with violation of the state law, Weyerhauser negotiated an agreement to purchase new equipment to eliminate sulfur dioxide releases by 1991. Until then, the gasses will not be released during recess time.

It is tempting to learn easy lessons from this case. To some, the case is evidence of the erosion of commitment to environmental and health regulation by the proindustry Reagan presidency. Some would seek more vigorous enforcement of rational and comprehensive regulations to prevent the risks of exposure to environmental hazards. To others, the case might illustrate a failure of overhead control as federal executive agencies seem to defy the purposes authorized and funded by Congress. They would seek more extensive legislative requirements, oversight activities, and evaluation research to assure that the purposes of the national legislature are faithfully carried out. But reality is complex and ambiguous.

The compromise solution indicates the values in conflict in this case and the diffuse distribution of authority (shared between levels of government and sectors of the political economy). Discharge of the gas continues to foul the area surrounding the plant, but the special damage caused by the proximity of the school to the plant has been mitigated somewhat by the agreement not to discharge during school recess. Production continues until new technology, the exact effect of which is not known, can be put in place. But even through compromise things change. As one Weyerhauser manager observed: "In the old days, people just lived with the discomfort they might get from the mill" (*The Washington Post,* 6/2/89, p. A8).

CORPORATE REGIME

The corporate regime—organized and operated along corporate lines while exercising public authority—is an implementation regime characterized by a diffusion of public authority within the joint action sector. In this context, the tension between centralized and diffuse authority is due to conflict over participation and control. The corporate regime exercises public authority but is subject to democratic control in only the most contrived circumstances. The tension between participation (an element of diffuse authority) and control (an element of centralized authority) is usually resolved in a manner that discounts the value of participation and emphasizes the importance of coherence and efficiency in policy implementation. Rhetorically, the emphasis upon control is linked to the concerns of the progressive movement for promotion of efficiency and effectiveness in public organizations (Stoker, 1987).

Organizations within a corporate regime often take a quasi-public form. This may be an intentional effort to create ambiguity in the public-private status of the organization which, in turn, benefits the organization and those who control it. Ambiguity allows those who seek autonomy and control of public policy to make convenient interpretations of their organization's status and legal rights or obligations (Stoker, 1987).

Given that it favors control over participation, this sort of regime is most appropriate for implementing policy that is consensual. An example of an argument to justify such a regime is found in Paul Peterson's *City Limits* (1981). Peterson argues that economic development problems in urban areas are consensus policies because economic growth is in everyone's interest. The problem, from this perspective, is that cities must compete for development investment. Therefore, the city that can most effectively limit demands from political representatives for consideration as a cost of implementing development policy will prevail in the competition.

Peterson's claims about development policy have been disputed. Clarence Stone (1987) has argued that it is unlikely that a singular, known interest exists for the city; what is more likely is that implementation participants interpret policy as they implement it, creating an interest for the city that reflects their position, interests, and beliefs. When this process is closed and quiet, as it is likely to be in a corporate regime, abuse of public authority is a possibility that cannot be ignored (Stone, 1980).

Corporate Politics in Baltimore

An example of a corporate regime is the implementation of economic development policy by Baltimore's shadow government.[5] Development policy in Baltimore historically has been made by institutions outside the city's administrative apparatus—a "shadow government" of quasi-public organizations and extragovernmental officials dominates the city's development agenda in a process that is "fluid, flexible, and ad hoc" (Stoker, 1987, p. 245).

An illustration of Baltimore's corporate regime at work is the use of federal Community Development Block Grants (CDBGs) to finance aspects of the construction of the Coldspring new town in Baltimore. Administered as a competitive, formula-based grant by the Department of Housing and Urban Development (HUD), CDBGs played a major role in the financing of Coldspring.

The original, ambitious plan for the Coldspring new town has been largely unfulfilled and, recently, the city has suggested a possible change in direction.[6] Among the many problems in implementing the new town initiative were construction deficiencies. The project's developer argued that the deficiencies resulted from substandard work done by minority contractors. (This claim had significant political implications for, like many urban communities, it was Baltimore's policy to promote the use of minority subcontractors on projects it sponsored. In essence, the developer was blaming the city for the problems.) The one million dollar cost to repair the deficiencies was covered by CDBGs. However, this failed to resolve the dispute between the developer and minority subcontractors. The subcontractors filed claims, clouding the title of prospective homeowners. To end the dispute, the city forgave $400,000 in loans that had been advanced by a city agency to the subcontractors, again financing the loss with CDBGs.

Problems with construction deficiencies in the Coldspring project were resolved by reaching into the deep pocket of the federal government. Responding to criticism of this use of federal funds, Lawrence Daley, then a city trustee and a major player in Baltimore's shadow government, argued that no harm was done: "That subsidy is not city funds. That's federal grants." (*Baltimore Sun,* 4/16/80, p. A1).

Jeffrey Henig (1985, pp. 184–85) observes that the emphasis placed upon local discretion in the block grant formulation of CDBGs implied increased discretion in the hands of local decision makers. Local discretion may allow those who are well positioned to dominate local development policy. Ironically, Henig reports that one argument used as justification for local discretion is that it makes policy deliberations more democratic by allowing local citizens to be involved in the process of determining the purposes of federal grants. But, absent federal provisions for participation (and lacking even clear criteria for targeting federal assistance), established local development leaders—who are insulated from political conflict within the city itself—may enjoy a good deal of discretion in the use of federal funds. The corporate regime is often an effective tool to this end.

QUASI MARKETS

There are two types of quasi-market regimes: one organized and directed by federal authority and the other based upon authority shared by federal, state, and local governments. The quasi-market regime attempts to establish a market for the production and distribution of a good or service that has not been spontaneously produced. This implies difficulty inasmuch as the market is valued for its productive efficiency and robustness, but the necessity of intervention by public authority suggests that the good or service is to be produced and distributed on a basis other than willingness and ability to pay. A primary concern for shaping quasi-market regimes is how to realize the value of the market while limiting the discipline of the price system.

PRIVATIZATION AND IMPLEMENTATION REGIMES

Recent emphasis upon "privatization" at all levels of government indicates the growing importance of market and quasi-market mechanisms to policy implementation. Privatization initiatives include deregulation of vast sectors of the economy, emphasis upon volunteerism in the production of public services, user fees charged to those who enjoy the benefits of government policy, contracting-out for goods and services required by or provided by government, renewed emphasis upon incentives in policy design, and the sale of government-owned enterprises. Each of these initiatives can be seen as an attempt to infuse the implementation process with the virtues of the market.

Given the vast scope of privatization initiatives, it is not surprising that definitions of the term vary. According to the Grace Commission, to privatize is "to provide services without producing them" (Kettl, 1988, p. 11). E. S. Savas (1987) has defined privatization as "the act of reducing the role of government, or increasing the role of the private sector, in an activity or in the ownership of assets" (p. 3). Peter Benda and Charles Levine (1988) have referred to privatization as "attempts to transfer governmental responsibilities to the private sector" which can take two forms: (1) withdrawal of government from certain activities and (2) reliance upon the private sector to produce what government provides (pp. 120–24). John Donahue (1989), who defines privatization as the "practice of delegating public duties to private organizations," has argued that two dimensions exist in the privatization decision. One is financing—who should pay for the good or service? The other is performance—should the good or service be produced by a governmental or nongovernmental organization? (p. 7).

The intersection of these dimensions creates a typology of public/private choice (presented in figure 11). Donahue (1989) explains that the northwest quadrant of the figure is what most of us think of as the government—goods or services financed collectively and produced by civil servants. The southeast quadrant is the market—individuals purchasing goods or services produced by private firms. The northeast and southwest quadrants represent possible hybrid forms of organization that combine elements of the public and private sectors (pp. 7–8). One possible form of privatization is the use of collective payments (tax revenues) by government to purchase goods or services from the private sector (for example, the purchase of police cars by local government). A second possible form of privatization is payment by individuals in exchange for specific goods or services produced by government (for example, the collection of user fees to defray the costs of operation and maintenance of public parks).

Privatization is often understood as a movement toward the market and, by implication, away from government. Savas (1987) directly equates the decline of the governmental sector with the rise of the nongovernmental (private) sector (p. 6). While this view is consistent with most definitions and many privatization initiatives, it can be deceptive if it is thought to imply that privatization is directly equated with a diminished

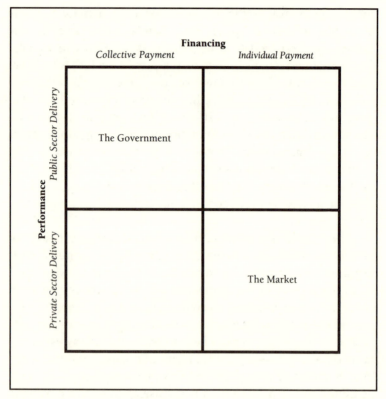

FIG. 11.   Dimensions of Public/Private Choice

role for bureaucracy and the realization of market efficiency. (Of course, some confusion about this matter is generated by advocates of privatization seeking to promote their cause by implying that to privatize is to substitute the efficiency and discipline of the market for the lethargy and ossification of bureaucracy).

To its advocates, privatization may seem a general solution to the problems of regime design and development—cooperation, accountability, efficiency, and control are realized when bureaucracy is circumvented by implementation strategies based upon market mechanisms.[7] According to this view, the federal government may improve its performance by employing profit-seeking agents to accomplish its ends. Enjoying the status of customer (and, due to its size and resources, exercising substantial market power to create economies of scale), the federal government can depend upon competition, the price system, and performance incentives inherent in the market to induce cooperation from its agents. If unsatisfied, the government may shop the market, seeking new agents to produce what it desires for a competitive price.

However, Donahue argues that the implications of privatization depend upon more than simple distinctions between the public and private sectors. The means by which government produces goods or services requires a choice between buying obedience to instruction (the employment relationship) and arranging for delivery of a product (the contractual relationship). What distinguishes one from the other is whether means (process) or ends (products) are specified and evaluated. For Donahue (1989), the significance of privatization is not in the choice of civil servants (public bureaucracy) or profit seekers (private firms), but in the choice to create competitive, output-based relationships or noncompetitive, input-based relationships (p. 82).

The Value of Privatization

Contracting in the market is generally preferred to employing civil servants for the production of goods and services to the extent that a task can be specified with precision in advance, accomplishment of goals is easily measured and evaluated, competition exists between profit-seekers, contractors can be easily replaced or penalized, and the concern of government focuses on ends, not means (Donahue, 1989, p. 97). In these circumstances, the opportunities for privatization are significant. Thus, the decision to privatize is a viable strategy for regime design.

The relevance of privatization to regime design is clear from the conception of political power that underlies the regime approach. If power is the capacity to act (following Stone, 1989), the capacity of the private sector (its expertise and control of resources) makes commercial interests attractive partners. In this sense, privatization can be seen as a practical response to the problem of governance in a liberal political economy—the characteristic diffusion of authority creates the need for government to engage the private sector in order to accomplish public purposes. If this is so, the political problems of regime design (in other words, who is empowered and with what consequences for evolution of policy during the implementation process) also are found when initiatives are implemented through privatization.

The value of privatization depends upon context and the importance of process. If uncertainty and risk are elements of the context in which policy is implemented, a contractual relationship is likely to focus on inputs and process rather than output and results. Donahue (1989) asserts that risk is an especially relevant concern. When risk is high, "the prudent agent may decline to enter into a purely output-based contract, or may demand a steep premium for accepting the risk. The principal, then, may do better to bear the risk himself, and to offer a contract paying the agent according to input rather than outputs" (p. 41).

Thus the nature of the relationship has changed fundamentally. No longer is it proper to think of the federal government as a customer purchasing goods or services in the marketplace. By contracting for inputs rather than outputs, the linkage between efficiency and accountability is jeopardized. Donahue (1989) warns that, "once the bond between payment and ultimate results is severed, the agency relationship is vulnerable to breakdown" (p. 41).

The breakdown is familiar to students of public policy. In his review of the effects of performance evaluation, V. F. Ridgeway has observed that, when agents are rewarded for input instead of output, or when they are evaluated on the basis of proxy measures of accomplishment, dysfunctional consequences may result (1983). Agents concentrate their efforts in order to maximize rewards even if this frustrates the intentions of the principal. (In the market such responsiveness to incentives is considered a virtue.) For example, when agents operating a job training program are rewarded for the number of participants who gain employment (a proxy measure of accomplishment), they are likely to "cream" the applicants, selecting program participants on the basis of their employability rather than their need for assistance. Instead of serving those in need, the incentive structure transforms the program into a placement service for those who would likely find employment on their own. In short, contractors may exhibit just the sort of troublesome behavior that advocates of privatization commonly associate with public bureaucracy.

The breakdown of the agency relationship implies an important conclusion: Privatization is not a general solution to the problems of regime design and development. The exception to this rule is when government does not care about process and can contract for outputs in a competitive environment.

From the regime perspective, the central task of the implementation process is to create institutions in order to induce cooperation in a mixed motive context. Rather than solving the problem of inducing cooperation from reluctant partners, privatization alters the nature of the regime and the dynamics that influence its development.

The Implications of Privatization

There are several aspects of privatization which affect the nature and development of the implementation regime. When profit seekers implement policy, lines of accountability may be blurred. This has implications for establishing legal and political responsibility for the content of policy. One advantage of public sector organizations is that they are accountable (through various direct and indirect means) to political authority. A key role for political leadership is to intervene on behalf of constituents who are dissatisfied with public services. This sort of accountability may be undermined when implementation is privatized.

The use of profit-seeking firms to implement policy may undermine accountability in two ways. First, procedures for oversight and evaluation, which are common in the public sector, are not as likely to be in place. There are fewer, less stringent requirements for public notice, participation, and openness. Though this may increase productive efficiency, it can also shield abuse. Second, information gathered and disseminated by profit seekers is not likely to facilitate the evaluation of performance and oversight. Transactions may be intentionally complex and records deliberately cryptic. Thus, it may be difficult, even with a substantial commitment of resources, to reconstruct a clear picture of responsibility. An example of privatized policy implementation that illustrates these dangers is the Iran-Contra affair.

Organizational norms are different in the private sector. Though advocates of privatization are likely to point to the virtues of profit seekers' industry and flexibility, it is nonetheless true that private sector organizations lack a public service ethos. They are more likely to view the implementation process opportunistically and contribute to the probability of exploitive behavior.

Examining the role of a small Kansas bank in the problems of the student loan program, the *Washington Post* (9/30/90, p. H1) reported that the Bank of Horton thrived on high-risk student loans (primarily loans to students attending trade schools). These loans were insured by the Higher Education Assistance Fund (HEAF) and guaranteed by the federal government. In 1988 the Bank of Horton was one of the leading originators of student loans in the United States and eventually also became a leader in some categories of default. As a consequence of insuring too many bad loans, many of which were originated by Horton, HEAF can no longer cover its financial obligations, triggering a federal bailout. However, Craig MacPherson, Horton's director, indicates that the bank acted properly: "If you see a niche in a government program run out of Washington, D.C., and you exploit that niche in an honest way, you're doing what Congress intended you to do" (p. H4).

Of course, a key to the effectiveness of privatization is the extent of competition among profit seekers. Competition is required to realize the benefits of market efficiency and innovation. But, even when the nature of competition is extensive, the passage of time may serve to limit it. Donahue (1989) argues that participation in the process of developing policy may provide advantages that undermine the competitive forces of the marketplace. As time goes by, the firm that is well positioned comes to enjoy advantages because it is familiar with the ways of doing business required by government, or advantageous information about the desires of the government has been revealed, or government becomes committed to the process as it is developed and gains acceptance (or popularity). If this is true, the value of market competition is undermined.[8]

When competition is limited initially, government is likely to view its agents in the marketplace as important sources of supply. In this circumstance, concerns other than productive efficiency may weigh heavily in contracting decisions. A familiar example is the military-industrial complex. Though technically private, firms that produce weapons systems are likely to depend upon government contracts for a substantial share of their business. Without these contracts, the firms would not remain viable. Recognizing this, and realizing the importance of the survival of the supplier, federal officials may be reluctant to infuse contractual relationships with too much of the discipline of the market. Such innovations as "cost-plus" contracts are the result.

Privatization is a viable regime design strategy, but should not be regarded as a general solution to the problems of inducing cooperation with reluctant partners. Movement from the governmental to the market action sector affects the nature of regime design and development, creating both opportunities and problems.

FEDERAL QUASI MARKET

The national government creates a quasi market by financing the purchase of services or goods from the private sector, resulting in a "federal quasi market." Sometimes private sector organizations serve as intermediaries between program participant(s) and the service-providing organization(s).

An example of a federal quasi market is the Guaranteed Student Loan Program, which provides loans for students who attend universities or other educational institutions eligible by federal standards. In this quasi-market system, banks serve as intermediaries who accept loan applications and assemble the documents required to demonstrate eligibility. Federal funding is provided on the basis of national income eligibility criteria to subsidize interest payments so long as the participant continues to be enrolled as a full-time student in good standing and to insure the bank's risk in making the loan. Following a grace period which begins when the student completes his program or stops attending school, loan repayment—principal and interest—becomes the student's responsibility.

To loan large amounts of money to young people, many of whom are not employed and have no established credit or collateral, is an unusual practice in the marketplace. Federal policy apparently mitigates the apprehension that the private sector would have in making such risky investments. This points to the contradiction at the core of the quasi-market regime. If the transaction could stand the rigors of the market place, a spontaneous order would be sufficient to provide it and public intervention would be needless. Public intervention often occurs because the market has failed to create desired outcomes or to serve some segment of the population.

By creating a national quasi market, the loan program frees students to select any eligible educational institution without concern for its quality or cost. Regardless of the student's decision, the same program standards apply and, regardless of cost, students are eligible for the same amount of federal support. It can be argued that the loan program has actually distorted the market for higher education services and contributed to steep increases in tuition. The availability of easy loan money that seems to have only distant costs may make students less price-sensitive in their consumption decisions. As a result, they may "overconsume" education services.

SHARED QUASI MARKET

An illustration of the shared quasi-market implementation regime is the Section 8 "Existing Housing Program" administered by the Department of Housing and Urban Development (HUD) and local housing authorities. Under the authority of the Housing and Community Development Act of 1974, the program sought to expand opportunities for the poor and near poor to participate in the rental housing market. The federal government was not to be involved in construction, ownership, or management of housing. Program benefits were provided directly to participants on the basis of a sliding scale that specified the percentage of the participant's income (possibly as much as 30%) that must be paid in rent. Federal rent subsidies—in the form of certificates—are provided to make up the difference between the rental cost charged by the private owner and the percentage of income paid by the participant toward rent. The use of certificates allows the participant to select the unit which best fits his needs from the local housing market.

The program is jointly administered by HUD and local public housing authorities. The federal government establishes standards for eligibility, specifies the rent share to be paid by program participants, develops standards for adequate housing, and finances the rent subsidy. Local authorities are responsible for assessing compliance with HUD standards and, most importantly, selecting the participants. Local selection of participants is made more important by the fact that many more people are eligible for program benefits than can be funded under current allocations for the program (Henig, 1985, p. 189).

Jeffrey Henig (1985) argues that an important difference between this program and more conventional housing programs is that the participants have "greater freedom" in selecting their dwelling. Rather than limiting participants to a project specifically constructed for low-income residents and operated by public officials, this program is designed to facilitate the participation of the poor and near poor in the rental market. This enhances the bargaining power of participants by affording them the ability to vote with their feet (p. 188).

CONCLUSION

Since the demise of the politics/administration dichotomy, analysts have been concerned about the political implications of administrative processes. But this concern has often focused primarily on who has been empowered and what specific authority has been granted. This chapter extends that concern to consider the implications of regime arrangements for governance. As Clarence Stone has noted, "Governing . . . does not require that a group be in command . . . but only that it be able to recast the terms on which key social transactions occur" (1987, p. 273).

To truly understand the politics of the implementation process we must look beyond the intentions of policy formulators and formal structures of empowerment to examine how the capacity to act is realized in governing arrangements (Stone, 1987). This chapter has explored some of the many means available to organize and exercise authority in the implementation process. Each regime type exhibits some aspect of the essential conflict that must be resolved in implementing national policy in a liberal, federal polity—the reconciliation of tension between centralized and diffuse authority. However, differences between the regime types are important because aspects of regime design affect the distribution of power and the development of the regime over time. As regime arrangements are devised and as policy evolves in response to the forces present in the regime, the capacity of government to act is both generated and limited (Stone, 1989).

5 POLICY REFORM AND IMPLEMENTATION PERFORMANCE

THE FEDERAL GOVERNMENT'S record of accomplishment has been uneven, suggesting that there remains much to learn about how to design effective national policy. However, one point is clear: The complex and dynamic nature of policy problems makes comprehensive policy design difficult, if not impossible. Change and adjustment are inevitable. The regime framework suggests that reforms introduced following a history of cooperation and policy coordination are more likely to be successfully implemented. This implies that effective policy making is best viewed as a process that requires periodic reconsideration and thoughtful reform.

In this chapter, the effects of policy reform over time upon program performance are explored through examination of the National School Lunch Program (NSLP). What emerges from this case is a pattern of responsiveness by implementors to changes in federal priorities and implementation standards—first to demands for wider, more liberal distribution of benefits and later to cutbacks attributed to the imperatives of the federal budget deficit.

From the regime perspective, the National School Lunch

Program (NSLP) is a significant case, for there are many reasons the program could have failed. The program broke new ground in an environment historically hostile to federal participation—education. Despite this, the program has forged constructive partnerships among federal, state, and local policy makers and has enjoyed positive evaluations. An understanding of how this was accomplished may provide important insights to those who design policy, reform it, or implement it with reluctant partners.

The NSLP also is an appropriate case for analysis, given that the research focuses on reformulation of federal policy over time. The NSLP has been implemented in three distinct phases, each phase defined by a series of program reforms indicating changes in federal priorities. What changes in the implementation process were required to successfully introduce these reforms? How did implementors respond to changing federal priorities? Is there evidence of changing program performance that reflects cooperation with changing federal priorities?

NATIONAL SCHOOL LUNCH ACT

According to the National School Lunch Act, the purpose of the National School Lunch Program is to safeguard the well-being of the nation's schoolchildren and to encourage the consumption of nutritious domestic agricultural commodities. These goals are to be accomplished through the establishment, maintenance, operation, and expansion of nonprofit school lunch programs. At the time the program was conceived, encouraging consumption of domestic foodstuff was considered an important national goal which would maintain the base of U.S. domestic agricultural production by protecting the price levels enjoyed by domestic producers. To use excess foods to provide lunches for the nation's schoolchildren seemed reasonable, and, in this context, the National School Lunch Program was born.

It is hazardous to infer the purposes of public policy formulators from their pronouncements—posturing is a frequent substitute for sincere statement of intent. However, it is plausible to assume that the purpose of the lunch program is to provide lunch services to school-age children at reduced costs. The program provides three separate categories of assistance, two of which are eligible for a special federal subsidy under Section 11 of the act. Students whose families fall within the income guidelines established by Congress may receive a free or reduced price meal. Other participants pay the regular price for their lunches.

The program has several components designed to facilitate the establishment and operation of lunch programs in local schools. The burden of finance is shared by the federal, state, and local authorities. States are required to match each federal dollar with three state dollars except for the special federal subsidy provided to free and reduced price participants (for which no matching funds are required). Schools receive a basic subsidy for all lunches that reduces the cost of a regular price meal. In addition to direct subsidies, the program provides commodities (or their cash equivalent) to participating schools. Initially, the secretary of the USDA was empowered to donate only food that could be purchased at surplus prices, but this authority was later revised to authorize not only the purchase of commodities in surplus, but also those needed to operate the program. Until recently, a component for capital development was included in the program to finance the establishment of the physical plant required to produce and distribute lunches in local schools.[1] Other provisions of the act defray the cost of state administration and sponsor nutrition education programs.

The program is to be operated through state education agencies, when feasible. If no such agency exists, or if the agency is unable to serve a given school in the state, the secretary of the USDA is authorized to administer the program directly.[2] The arm of the USDA responsible for program administration is the Food and Nutrition Service (FNS). Regional offices of the FNS are charged with program management. Working through state agencies, school districts contract with the FNS to provide lunch services that meet minimum standards established by USDA regulations and congressional mandate. Lunch policies that are not otherwise specified are the purview of the local school authorities. The Commodity Credit Corporation (CCC) is also involved in the lunch program through the purchase and distribution of foodstuff. Thus, the typical administrative structure of the lunch program involves at least six organizational actors: the secretary of the USDA, the FNS, the CCC, regional offices of the FNS, state education agencies, and local school authorities. Others who have historically been influential in program administration or evaluation include key members of congressional committees (especially the Education and Labor Committee of the House of Representatives and the Select Committee on Nutrition and Human Needs of the U.S. Senate), the General Accounting Office, the inspector general of the USDA, state auditors, local parent's associations, teacher's organizations, child or nutrition advocacy groups, and vendors of lunch services.

PHASES OF PROGRAM DEVELOPMENT

Although the ostensible purpose of the lunch program is to provide lunch services to students, the program's character has changed over time by placing more or less emphasis on this goal. It can be argued that the NSLP has gone through three stages since its inception (see figure 12). Each of the stages is distinguished from the others by a series of key program reforms.

To divide the program's history into such distinct phases is somewhat deceptive. While each date represents a significant and symbolic development in the NSLP, a more accurate appraisal would reveal a slow transformation of the program from one phase to another. The changes also mark the rise and decline of emphasis placed upon different aspects of the program's many possible objectives. In the first phase, the program was implemented in a manner reflecting the historic mission of the USDA and the interests of its traditional constituency in managing the agricultural economy. Indeed, the very fact that the USDA was selected as the federal program sponsor speaks volumes about the priority of child nutrition. The emphasis of the

Constituent Phase 1947	Progressive Phase 1966	Budget Conscious Phase 1980
Initiated as a contituent program for USDA	Program becomes more socially progressive as benefits increase	Deficit requires benefit and eligibility changes

FIG. 12. Evolution of the NSLP

program as a tool to help manage the agricultural sector of the economy diminished somewhat in the second phase as the program was expanded to place more emphasis on serving the nutritional needs of students. Especially important to this change was the rise of concern for students who had in the past been overlooked or ill-served by the lunch program—the poor and near poor. In the third phase federal priorities again shifted to emphasize reductions in program expenditures through tighter control of eligibility requirements, closer accounting of program expenditures, and elimination of some program benefits.

These changes are relevant to the regime framework because they mark significant alterations of the purposes of federal policy. To accomplish changes in program performance consistent with their changing priorities, federal policy makers must gain the cooperation of implementors at the state and local levels. In the following sections, the phases of program development and reform are described.

THE CONSTITUENT PHASE, 1947–1966

The initial stage of the NSLP could be called the "constituent phase" because many aspects of the program implied subordination of the goal of child nutrition to service to the constituents of the USDA. During this period federal support for the establishment and operation of the program was limited. Increases

in participation actually outpaced the growth in federal support
so that benefit levels were reduced.[3] The benefits that were provided consisted only of donated surplus commodities and the
basic lunch subsidy. There was no federal support for free or
reduced price lunches and no funding was available as seed
money to establish lunch programs. The absence of these services severely limited participation options for poorer children
who were less likely to attend schools with adequate physical
plants and less able to afford lunches that were available to them
at regular prices.

The primacy of constituent concerns also is indicated by the
role of the Commodity Credit Corporation. The authority provided by the Congress allowed only the purchase of commodities that were in surplus for donation to the schools. This meant
that schools were likely to receive commodity donations on an
unreliable schedule and that the content of program commodity
donations was driven by the ups and downs of agricultural supply rather than the needs of the lunch program.

It should come as no surprise that the program received
mixed reviews during this initial period. Participants in the program did enjoy the benefits of improved nutritional well-being,
but, in terms of satisfying the nutritional need of children na-
tionwide, poor participation rates indicated that program success was limited. One of the most compelling criticisms of the
program was that many eligible children were unwilling or unable to participate.

After twenty years of service, participation rates nationally
(reported in table 1) indicate the program was a mixed success.
In 1947, more than six million children (22 percent) participated in the program. Over the next twenty years, participation
increased to more than 18.8 million (36 percent). In 1947, 24
percent of eligible schools elected to participate; by 1967, this
proportion had increased to 60.9 percent. Despite this growth,
it seems strange that nearly 40 percent of schools and more than
60 percent of students remained nonparticipants after twenty
years of what had been essentially a distributive program.

Several flaws in the NSLP were seen as obstacles to increas-

TABLE 1
NSLP Participation Over Time

	Students (in thousands)	(%)	Schools	(%)
1947	6,014	22.4	44,542	24.0
1952	9,794	29.8	56,851	33.1
1957	11,492	30.5	57,261	38.9
1962	14,957	33.1	66,715	49.6
1967	18,800	36.7	71,983	60.9

Sources: USDA and FNS reports. Percent calculations were developed from estimates of national school enrollments and number of schools from various education surveys. Unless otherwise noted, national participation figures include all states and territories of the United States and the District of Columbia. The variable "Years" indicates the year of the start of the school year; for example, 1952 indicates the 1952–53 school year, not the federal fiscal year.

ing participation among students and schools. One was the disbursement formula. Critics claimed that the formula contained in the initial legislation was flawed and provided incentives contrary to expansion of the program. The formula distributed monies to states based upon the number of school-age children and the per capita income of the state. Two states with similar numbers of children and similar incomes would receive the same amount of federal support regardless of their participation rates. This arrangement was a boon to states with lower participation rates as they would receive more funds per student participant than states with higher rates.

Another criticism of the program was the lack of federal guidelines and support for free and reduced price lunches, since states could provide such services at their discretion and expense. During the initial period, participation among free and reduced price students accounted, on the average, for only about 11 percent of total participation. (The proportion of free and reduced price participants actually decreased from a high of 16.6 percent in 1950, to about 10 percent throughout the early 1960s.) In sum, the program's initial phase could be characterized as a mixed success since elements of the program seemed to deemphasize the importance of child nutrition. Though many students participated and benefited from the program, especially troubling were the limited opportunities for participation among the poor and near poor.

THE PROGRESSIVE PHASE, 1967–1980

The second phase of the NSLP could be called the "progressive phase" because, during this period, the goal of child nutrition was promoted through several key reforms, including liberalization of eligibility standards, development of nonfood assistance programs, and extension of the authority of the CCC to purchase commodities. Although the groundwork for this transition was established in the early 1960s, 1966 was the watershed year because both the character and process of program funding were changed.

In 1961, federal expenditures for free and reduced price lunches were first authorized. In fiscal year 1966, funds were first appropriated for this purpose. In 1962, the disbursement formula for distributing funds among the states was altered to encourage comprehensive participation. The revised formula distributed money on the basis of the number of participants in the state and per capita income. This change was phased in over four years (from 1962 to 1966).

Federal support for the program increased dramatically during the progressive phase. In table 2, the amount of total federal grants to states is reported. From an initial value of $141 million in 1965, federal grants increased more than ten times to $1,491 million by 1975.

Much of the growth in federal spending occurred as increased assistance for free and reduced price participants through Section 11 funding. The growth in Section 11 funding indicates increasing opportunities for needy children to take advantage of NSLP benefits. By 1980, Section 11 funds represented nearly 50 percent of total federal contributions to the program. Given

TABLE 2
Federal Grants to NSLP

Year	Total (in millions)	Biennial Growth Rate
1965	141.090	—
1967	159.754	.132
1969	300.258	.880
1971	738.764	1.460
1973	1,085.314	.469
1975	1,491.544	.374

Source: FNS report series SL-5.

this change, it is not surprising that the program experienced growth in the form of serving more free and reduced price lunches. In table 3 the percentage of NSLP participants who received free or reduced price lunches is presented. Section 11 participation rates for the first twenty years were typically 10 to 11 percent. However, by 1980, Section 11 participants represented more than 45 percent of total student participation.[4]

Other program reforms also were enacted during the progressive phase. To encourage participation among children, competitive foods were regulated and nutrition education programs were developed. Federal eligibility guidelines for Section 11 participation created uniform national standards for free and reduced price lunches. Capital development initiatives allowed less affluent schools to develop the physical plant required to offer NSLP service. The authority of the CCC was revised to allow the purchase of commodities needed to operate the program—not just commodities in surplus.

These program reforms had an effect. Evaluations of the program contended that its performance had improved. In a nutritional survey of ten states, the Department of Health, Education, and Welfare[5] reported that the NSLP was an important part of the daily nutrition of many children—especially low-income and minority children.[6] Similar conclusions were reached by the General Accounting Office (GAO). GAO's major conclusion was the "NSLP has been effective in increasing both

TABLE 3
Percentage of Free and Reduced Price Participants

Year	Percent
1960	10.1
1965	10.9
1970	26.1
1975	43.1
1980	48.6

Sources: USDA and FNS reports.

the nutrient intakes and the quality of food consumed by the participants." Beyond this, the income-poverty guidelines used by USDA to target the program are "the best available means for targeting NSLP."[7]

Despite these positive results, the program did not escape controversy. The dissatisfaction surrounding the NSLP is based not so much on its failure to achieve the stated objective as it is in fraud and other behavior which has resulted in unwarranted expenditures. Concern over waste, fraud, and abuse was fueled by evaluation research that focused upon the management problems created by the high level of local discretion in program administration.

THE SCHOOL LUNCH MANAGEMENT CONTROVERSY

Audit research, conducted by the inspector general of the USDA, identified three types of recurring management problems in the NSLP, including invalid applications for program benefits, inflated meal counts for reimbursement, and unsupported per meal reimbursement rates.[8] This continuing controversy is based not so much on the program's effectiveness as on its efficiency. Few would argue that the NSLP has not contributed substantially to the nutrition of the nation's schoolchildren. Rather, the focus of criticism has been that, with more careful program management, cost reductions could be realized while maintaining present benefit levels.

Audit Review of the NSLP

The most common complaint contained in the audit review of the NSLP was that eligibility decisions made at the local level were flawed. Local officials have the authority to make such determinations, but are to do so in compliance with federal regulations. Audits discovered cases in which the eligibility of participants was not "properly established." Four different types of eligibility problems were identified: not all students receiving program benefits had an application on file; some applications on file were invalid on their face; erroneous classification decisions were made by local school officials; and improper "blanket" verifications were made (for example, local school officials had improperly verified all foreign and foster children for maximum program benefits).

A second set of problems discussed in the inspector general's report were improper reimbursement claims for NSLP meals. This problem was rooted in inaccurate meal counts that sometimes resulted in reimbursement for meals that failed to meet NSLP standards. Inaccurate methods used to count meals included claiming all applicants on file for reimbursement, claiming all applicants in attendance for reimbursement, improper meal counting techniques (including reimbursement for à la carte services and other meals that failed to meet minimum USDA standards for content), and claims for reimbursement which exceeded even the number of qualified applicants in attendance or on file.

Finally, the inspector general reported poor or inaccurate local accounting procedures that resulted in excessive per meal reimbursement rates. Sources of this problem included improper treatment of overhead expenses (for example, a disproportionate share, or sometimes all, of the indirect costs of food service were charged as program expenses); charges for the "expense" of commodities donated by the CCC; use of donated commodities for non-NSLP lunches (à la carte services or adult lunches); improper accounting of equipment costs (including both direct costs and depreciation as program expenses); improper inclusion of teacher's salaries, retirement pay, or benefits as program costs; and improper charges for donated milk as NSLP expenses. The most bizarre example in the category was a charge of six hundred dollars to the program by one local school that was then given to a student group. The school administration included this as a program expense when federal regulations regarding competitive food services required that a soda machine (which had been a source of revenue to the student group) be removed from the lunchroom.

The inspector general's report asserted that the NSLP had significant management problems because the program was not properly administered by state and local officials. During the progressive phase, efforts to expand program services often subordinated concern for efficient management. The policy of permitting local authorities to make eligibility decisions and verify them only "for cause" is one example. This policy, in effect, allowed local officials to use their discretion, including knowledge of their students not provided on program application forms, to make eligibility decisions. Though defensible as a use of local knowledge to improve policy, the practice of loose eligibility guidelines and local discretion represents a loss of federal control. As the political sands shift to emphasize efficiency and cost control, this sort of discretion is a likely target for reform.

The most recent program history is a significant reformulation for addressing management concerns and reducing federal expenditures. Through the budgetary process, the federal government has restricted eligibility, reduced financial support, and asserted oversight authority.

THE BUDGET CONSCIOUS PHASE, 1980–1990

Audit reports from 220 randomly selected schools, conducted by the inspector general of the USDA in May 1980, indicated that 30 percent of the applications for student participation were invalid or improperly verified. Projecting this error rate across the program, it was estimated that the federal cost of these errors was as much as $171.5 million during the 1979–80 school year.[9] It was argued that, through more careful administration, expenses could be cut without benefit losses. Advocates of the changes argued that their intent was to put limited resources where they were needed most—assistance for the needy. But opponents responded that the cutbacks would erode the financial and political base upon which the program depended. Major changes in the lunch program were enacted as provisions of the Omnibus Budget Reconciliation Act of 1981. The Reagan administration sought to reduce federal budgetary outlays, arguing that only the fat was being trimmed from federal programs—the "social safety net" would be retained. The reforms were presented as a way to concentrate scarce resources where they were most essential—in serving the poor.

Various provisions of the 1981 budget act reduced federal contributions or imposed hierarchical control upon local school officials. Key program reforms included new eligibility guidelines, reduced commodity contributions, disqualification of certain schools from participation, and a requirement for more data (and verification by local officials of the data provided) to gain eligibility for free or reduced price lunches. However, at the same time, federal reimbursement rates for free and reduced price participants who remained eligible under the new federal guidelines were increased. This allowed the Reagan administration to deflect criticism that maintained the cuts were hurting the poor. To the contrary, the administration's reforms placed opponents in the difficult position of opposing changes that placed greater emphasis upon the redistributive aspects of the NSLP.

The budget act tightened federal standards for determination of NSLP eligibility. In response, new regulations were developed in 1982 and 1983 that required that any student receiving program benefits have a completed, correct application for program benefits on file. Students lacking such documentation were not permitted to have lunch. Beyond this, schools districts were required to verify the income data provided on applications for 3 percent or three thousand of their participants (whichever was less). Prior to this time, schools were directed only to verify eligibility data for cause. For the first time, schools were directed to refuse benefits to any student who did not provide the required information.

CHANGING FEDERAL RELATIONS

Federal demands in the budget conscious phase have placed school administrators in the difficult position of policing the benefits their students receive. Changes in federal program standards have created some disturbing incidents. A series of newspaper articles described the scene at a Brooklyn school when several students were refused lunch because they lacked a proper application. Rather than allow the students to go hungry, the lunch program administrators collected the plate waste from other lunches and served it to the ineligible students.[10] Local program administrators are thus caught in the middle of increased conflict over the purpose and content of the program.

Responding to Federal Demands

Audit reports from the state of Ohio indicate changes in response to federal concerns, but also indicate the limits of authority and control in the implementation process. The stated objective of the audit is "to determine if the School District complied with applicable federal and state regulations." This is to be decided on the basis of an audit test that samples the free and reduced price applications on file to determine their "validity" and "if there were enough applications on file to support meals served." Tests are also conducted for "proper content and quality in lunches served," for lunchroom expenditures, lunchroom receipts, and budgetary procedures. The procedures for determining eligibility for free or reduced price lunches are described as follows:

> To apply for free or reduced-price benefits, households should
> fill out the application and return it to the principal's office. . . .
> A complete application is required. Households should answer
> all questions on the application. The following information
> must be provided: the food stamp case number for the house-
> hold or *both* the monthly amount and source of income for each
> household member *and* the total household monthly income,
> the names of all household members, the social security number
> of all household members 21 years or older or state that a
> household member does not have one, and the signature of an
> adult household member. If any of this information is missing,
> the school cannot process the application. (Ohio audit packet)

Parents are informed of the school's decision by letter, indicating the status of the application (approved for free lunch,
approved for reduced price lunch, or denied) and, if applicable,
the reason for denial. A sample letter included in the audit
packet advises parents, "If your child is approved for meal benefits, you must tell the school when your household income
increases by more than $50 per month ($600 per year) or when
your household size decreases." How this requirement is to be
enforced is not specified.

School districts are directed to verify the eligibility of applicants each year. The audit procedure to check compliance
with this requirement reviews applications on file and deter-
mines their validity. The number of valid applications on file
serves as a benchmark for evaluation of the legitimacy of reimbursement requests: if the number of reimbursements does not
exceed the number of applications on file, the school's performance is deemed satisfactory. To test for adequate meal content,
menus are obtained and reviewed to determine if they have the
right mix of components. This information is supplemented by
firsthand observation of "quantities" served to students.

The audit information is adequate to address the most obvious cases of waste, fraud, and abuse; however, the availability
of information and audit procedures severely limits the scope
of conclusions. In spite of these limits, evidence suggests that
federal concern for closer accountability has filtered down to

the state and local level. This has created tension between state auditors—the street-level bureaucrats charged with enforcing federal policy—and local school administrators. As one Ohio auditor said, "When I walk in [to conduct an audit], half of them are afraid of me. By the time I leave, they all are."

REGIME PERSPECTIVE ON THE NSLP

The program history presented here indicates that two significant reformulations of the NSLP have occurred. The purpose of this research is to establish whether or not implementation participants have been responsive to changing federal priorities. Since substantial changes in federal priorities have occurred, an important test of state and local cooperation is the extent to which indicators of program performance change following observed changes in priorities. For the transition from the constituent to the progressive phase, responsiveness would be indicated by increased participation across the board, but especially among those who were qualified for free or reduced price lunches. For the transition from the progressive to the budget-conscious phase, responsiveness would be indicated by reductions in participation among students and schools. (Although it is unclear whether the federal government had a hidden agenda for reducing student participation in the NSLP, case evidence indicates that the goal of student participation was subordinated to closer accountability during the budget-conscious phase.)

Were program reforms related to changes in selected measures of program performance? To answer this question, ARIMA models have been developed, with intervention terms representing the program reform initiatives previously described. (This technique is appropriate for time series analysis. For an overview of the process of the analysis, see Cook and Campbell, 1979, chap. 6).[11]

PRESENTATION OF FINDINGS

In figure 13 data regarding participation decisions among schools (measured as a percentage of all schools) is presented. If program reforms have been successfully implemented, changes in program performance consistent with the changing priorities of the federal government should be evident. In the case of school participation, the data should indicate two changes; an increase, in response to the priority given to increased partici- pation in the late 1960s, and a decrease, in response to federal cutbacks in the 1980s.

The data indicate that school participation increased during the progressive phase. In 1966, the school participation rate was 57.8 percent. By 1980 it had increased to more than 85 percent. In 1971, a positive, statistically significant change in slope oc- curred in the school participation series.[12] This result is espe- cially significant in light of the fact that most participation decisions represent the reversal of many years of nonpartici- pation. Following the initiation of the budget conscious phase, declines in participation among schools are evident. However, the decline in school participation in 1982 is not statistically significant (though it just missed the cutoff: T value −1.91). This result may be due to the relatively few observations avail- able for analysis.

However, gains in school participation are of little value if students fail to take advantage of the opportunity for NSLP ser- vice. It is important also to examine student participation. Stu- dent participation (whether measured as millions of students or as a proportion of total enrollment) indicated two statistically significant changes in response to changing federal priorities (see figures 14 and 15). In 1969, student participation increased (measured as the number of participants, the increase was a step function, but measured as a proportion it was a change in slope). In 1981, student participation declined as a step function for both measures. The direction of change and statistical signifi- cance of the findings indicates that changes in student partici- pation are consistent with changing federal priorities.

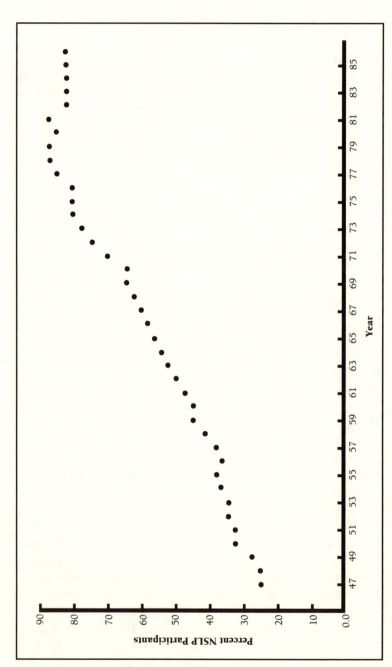

FIG. 13. School Participation in NSLP

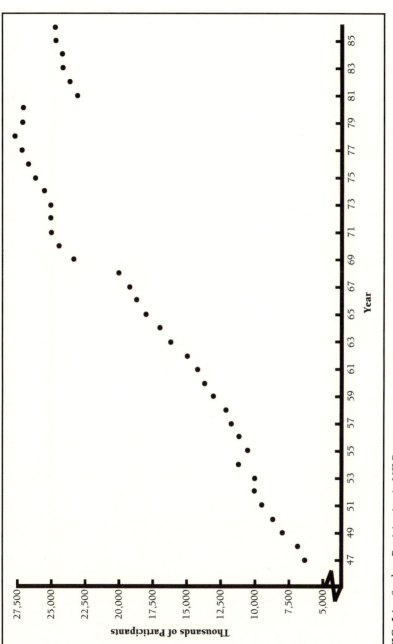

FIG. 14. Student Participation in NSLP

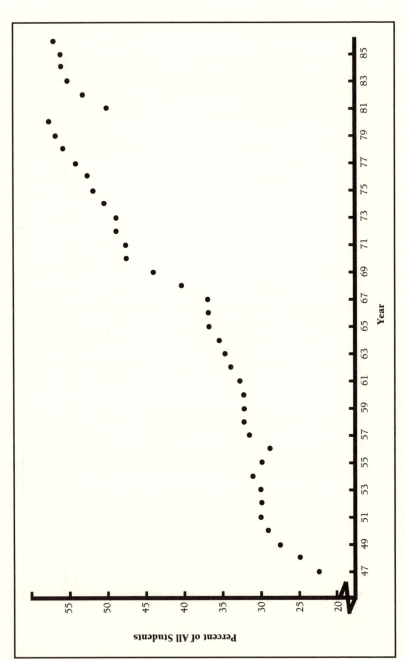

FIG. 15. Percent Student Participation in NSLP

The final measure of program performance is the proportion of free and reduced price participants. One clear goal of the progressive phase was to increase service to these students by enhancing their opportunity to participate in the lunch program. If states and localities cooperated with this change, increases in the proportion of participants in the free and reduced price categories would be evident following the reform. No statistically significant intervention term was found in the analysis.[13] However, this result is likely an artifact of method that is not substantively important. The data (presented in figure 16) indicate a clear pattern of exponential growth in free and reduced price participation beginning in the late 1960s.

Summary of Findings

The results of the analysis indicate that the program did exhibit substantial changes in performance following the initiation of federal program reforms (see table 4). For all of the results presented, the relationships are in the expected directions and are statistically significant. In short, the evidence indicates a pattern of covariation between the changes in federal priorities and

TABLE 4
Changes in NSLP Performance

Variable	Year of Change	Type of Change	T-Test	Regression Factor
Student participation				
Number	1969	step	4.69	1606
(in millions)	1981	step	−10.87	−3718
Percent	1969	slope	2.16 (NUM)	.0206
			15.62 (DEN)	.9407
	1981	step	−7.98	−.0842
School participation	1971	slope	3.23 (NUM)	.0502
			3.45 (DEN)	.696
Free and reduced price participation				
	no significant intervention			

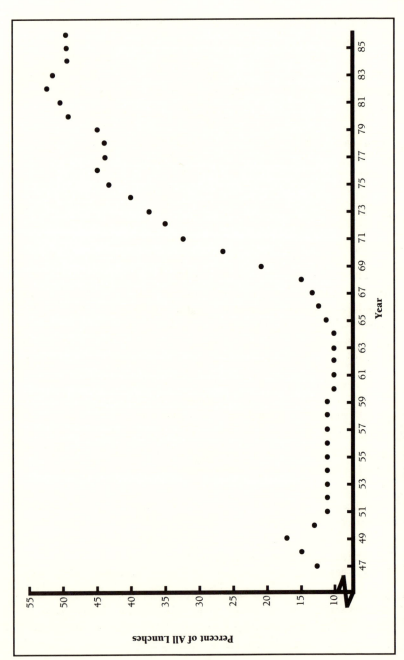

FIG. 16. Percent Free and Reduced Price Participation

program performance nationally.[14] Analysis of the residual term for each model is presented in the technical appendix to this chapter.

Interpretation of the Findings

There are many reasons why the NSLP might not have worked. Perhaps no domain of public affairs was more hostile to active federal participation than education. Yet the program forged a working partnership between state, local, and federal decision makers. Though the use of intermediaries has often been linked with implementation failure, the NSLP experienced growth and positive evaluations despite its emphasis upon federalism and diffuse implementation authority.

The regime framework would suggest that the initial suspicion of federal participation in education policy was mitigated by federalism—the provision of significant discretion to state and local decision makers. By placing emphasis on distributing program benefits in an atmosphere that emphasized participation over close accounting, potential conflict was avoided and the federal government was able to use existing state agencies and local education institutions effectively as intermediaries.

Success breeds success. By overcoming the initial obstacles to implementation, a history of cooperation was generated which later allowed the federal government to redirect the program in response to its changing priorities. In the mid-1960s the federal government emphasized social welfare objectives and caused states and localities to alter their practices so as to better serve the poor and near poor. Demands by the federal government to serve welfare objectives would have been more controversial had they not come within the context of success that the program had already established.

Of course, it could be argued that the outcome of the progressive reforms was predictable from the perspective of the exchange paradigm. Reflecting on the political dispositions of local school officials, their cooperation could be interpreted (following the exchange paradigm) as an indication of an absence of conflict. However, the second wave of federal reform, in the early 1980s, is inconsistent with the "no conflict" explanation. When program changes implied cutbacks that implicitly criticized local school officials and reduced their authority, cooperation was required from those who bore the cost of reform. In spite of the inherent limits of overhead control (see the discussion of the bureaucratic regime in chapter 4), evidence suggests that state and local officials cooperated with federal demands for closer program accountability.

One reason why implementors may be inclined to cooperate despite the need to absorb the costs of reform may be found in issue linkage. Program reform is an implicit issue linkage in as much as the continuation of the program becomes contingent upon the satisfaction of new requirements. The strategic situation is complex. Implementors are not offered all choices in a perfect world. They must make do with choices structured by program reform initiatives. This sometimes requires that they accept some bad (increased accountability) to maintain the good that the program is contributing (service to students). In this sense, reform, even reform that imposes costs, is less likely to generate opposition when a history of cooperation exists.

CONCLUSION

Evidence presented from the National School Lunch Program indicates that federal reforms have been effectively implemented. By creating a history of cooperation, federal policy makers were able to change the practices and performance of state and local implementors to make them consistent with changing federal objectives. This suggests that program reform is an important source of federal effectiveness. However, in spite of evidence that program reforms can also impose unwanted restrictions upon implementors, a fair criticism of this case is that it focuses upon a policy that is essentially distributive. Not all policy alternatives can distribute gains; some must impose costs. The problem of imposing costs is considered in the following chapter as the volatile issue of nuclear waste disposal is considered.

APPENDIX
Technical Appendix:
Model Specifications and Residual Analysis

Using SAS/ETS conditional least squares estimation, four AR-IMA models were estimated with intervention terms corresponding to the periods of program reform. In the tables below, the type and order of ARIMA process are specified and residual information is provided. The residual analysis is a test of the null hypothesis that the residuals are unpatterned, "white" noise, performed at various lag values. The higher the probability value associated with the Chi square test, the more likely is the null hypothesis. In all cases, the residual analysis indicated acceptance of the null hypothesis.

			Chi Square Test	
Variable	*ARIMA Model*	*Lag*	*Chi Square*	*Prob*
Percent	AR1	6	4.73	.449
Free and		12	8.08	.706
Reduced		18	9.35	.929
		24	18.51	.729

			Chi Square Test	
Variable	*ARIMA Model*	*Lag*	*Chi Square*	*Prob*
Percent Students	AR1	6	2.56	.768
		12	5.47	.906
		18	12.04	.797
		24	21.05	.578

			Chi Square Test	
Variable	*ARIMA Model*	*Lag*	*Chi Square*	*Prob*
Percent Schools	AR2	6	1.81	.771
		12	8.65	.565
		18	11.73	.762
		24	16.65	.782

			Chi Square Test	
Variable	*ARIMA Model*	*Lag*	*Chi Square*	*Prob*
Students in Millions	AR1	6	6.85	.232
		12	10.35	.499
		18	13.43	.707
		24	18.84	.711

6   NOT IN MY BACKYARD

OF THE PROBLEMS that confront national policy makers in a liberal, federal polity, perhaps none is more difficult than the implementation of a policy that imposes costs. In a context of diffuse authority, political and economic arrangements provide frequent opportunities to block public initiatives (through the courts, congressional intervention, public participation, or state and local resistance). This can make it difficult for society to address important problems of the day, especially if those whose cooperation is required stand to lose from the implementation of the policy.

To some in the popular press, the inability of government to resolve pressing social problems, or even to reach consensus about what to try next, has become so serious that they wonder "Is Government Dead?" (*Time,* 10/23/89). From homelessness to the federal budget deficit, government seems to be in retreat, with little evidence that other social institutions can fill the void. A common thread in these reviews of the ineffectual nature of government is the inability of the political system to impose costs: upon voters (such as a tax increase to reduce the federal deficit); upon key interest groups (recall the outcry among segments of the elderly population in response to the federal surtax to finance catastrophic health care, resulting in its repeal); or even upon the institutions of government itself (the difficulties of implementing spending restraint in the Pentagon were evident recently when Congress overruled military planners to finance construction of fighter planes the military had said it did not need).

This chapter tackles the difficult problem of imposing costs in a context of diffuse authority. It is relatively easy to formulate and implement policy that is distributive, since everyone gains from the policy, reducing opposition during the implementation process (recall the discussion of the relationship between cooperation and conflict of interest in chapter 3). However, not all policy initiatives can distribute gains. What hope, if any, exists for implementing policy in a context of diffuse authority when those who participate in the implementation process seek to avoid or minimize the costs associated with the decision?

Many contemporary policy issues could have been selected to illustrate this problem, but perhaps none so clearly crystalizes the problem of imposing costs as the disposal of nuclear waste. This problem's sources are multiple and amorphous. Historically a policy arena of extensive federal involvement, the costs (both actual and perceived) of resolving the problem are immediate and threatening. No other policy area is as likely to engender such spirited opposition—even hysteria—from the public. As the federal government struggles to implement policy to manage nuclear waste, citizens have sent a clear message to public officials: "Not in my backyard."

THE PROBLEM OF NUCLEAR WASTE

Nuclear waste is developed as a by-product of nuclear technologies for weapons development, energy production, academic research, commercial research and production, and medical applications. In part, the problem of nuclear waste is a legacy of attempts by the federal government to promote the use of atomic technology following the Second World War. The Atomic Energy Act of 1954 proclaimed: "Atomic energy is capable of application for peaceful as well as military purposes" and sought to facilitate the development of atomic energy to contribute to the general welfare but noted that national defence was "the paramount objective."

Among the provisions of the act were the creation of the Atomic Energy Commission (AEC) and the congressional Joint Committee on Atomic Energy. Walter Rosenbaum (1987) reports that the effect of these provisions was to create a sympathetic subgovernment that initially dominated federal nuclear policy. The AEC, together with the Joint Committee on Atomic Energy, provided a supportive environment for the promotion of nuclear technology that included various sorts of federal subsidies, such as underwriting research and development costs, provision of fuel for civilian reactors, and shared patents (p. 136) But, while encouraging the development of nuclear industries, the act made no provisions for repositories for nuclear waste.

Key Participants in the Implementation Process

For a time the atomic subgovernment was a stable coalition in favor of expanding the nuclear industry, but major transformations of the initial participants in the atomic subgovernment occurred in the 1970s. The Nuclear Regulatory Commission (NRC) was established in 1974 by the Energy Reorganization Act to replace the AEC as the lead federal agency regulating nuclear industries. The NRC assumed responsibility for the licensing, construction, and operation of nuclear reactors and other nuclear facilities, as well as the transportation and disposal of nuclear waste (Rosenbaum, 1987, p. 143).

The Department of Energy (DOE) was created as a cabinet level department in 1977. The DOE has authority relevant to energy policy issues, including nuclear waste management programs. The DOE implemented the Waste Isolation Pilot Project (WIPP) and has been the lead federal agency in the selection process for potential sites to locate the nation's high-level nuclear waste repositories, under provisions of the Nuclear Waste Policy Act of 1982.

Changes in other policy realms also have affected nuclear waste disposal, specifically the rise and institutionalization of the environmental movement in the United States. Federal requirements for consideration of the environmental impact of construction and for protection of endangered species have often been key areas of dispute in nuclear policy, especially as it relates to nuclear waste. Among the most important federal legislation for its effect on the nuclear industry was the National Environmental Policy Act which expanded the regulatory burden of the nuclear industry to include the Environmental Protection Agency (EPA) and required consideration of the environmental impact of nuclear activities.

Types of Nuclear Waste

Although there are a variety of different sorts of nuclear waste, precise distinctions between types is sometimes difficult. Hiskes and Hiskes (1986, pp. 93–97) list six different waste classifications: uranium mill tailings, low-level waste, transuranic waste, spent fuel waste, high-level waste, and decommissioning waste. Mill tailings are a by-product of the generation of fuel-grade uranium. The least radioactive of all types of nuclear waste, mill tailings are the greatest source of waste in volume. Low-level waste is a broad, residual category that comes from many different sources. Transuranic elements are those that have an atomic number higher than uranium; transuranic waste is associated with these elements. Spent fuel waste consists of uranium pellets rods used as fuel for nuclear reactors. Though not officially designated as waste, storage of spent fuel rods is a growing problem as many are currently in "temporary" storage in pools of water at nuclear installations. Decommissioning waste is associated with the disposal of nuclear reactors themselves. Reactors from electrical generating plants or nuclear powered ships that have outlived their utility (usually no more than forty years), must be disposed of. The DOE has completed the first disposal of a decommissioned reactor by encasing the reactor vessel in concrete and hauling it by barge from its former location (in Pennsylvania) to a burial site on the federal nuclear reservation in Hanford, Washington.

Public Perception of the Problem

There is no matter of public policy that generates more fear and apprehension on the part of the public than issues dealing with nuclear technology. In part this may reflect the history of nuclear policy in which federal officials (or contractors supervised by federal officials) have seemed to have insufficient concern about protecting the safety and well-being of people living near nuclear facilities (see, for example, Steele, 1988, 1989; *Time,* 10/31/88). Highly publicized accidents such as Three Mile Island or Chernobyl may also contribute to public perception of the risks of nuclear technology.

An analysis of risk perception found that when compared to a diverse list of activities and technologies nuclear technology scored highest on the most salient dimension of risk—"dread risk" (Slovic, 1987). Dread risk indicates a perceived lack of control with the possibility of fatal, catastrophic consequences that are inequitably distributed. A second dimension of risk, "unknown risk," indicates that a hazard is perceived to be unobservable, unknown, and delayed in consequence. Radioactive waste was the lowest scoring nuclear activity on dread risk (but still was higher on this dimension than all other activities and technologies except for nerve gas accidents), but highest among all nuclear activities on unknown risk (Slovic, 1987). In short, public perception of the risk from nuclear waste is high.

An analysis of risk perception that compared public decision makers and private citizens in Pennsylvania found that differences exist in the perceived risk from nuclear waste dumps (Bord, 1987). The general public perceived the risks to be greater than did selected public decision makers and the public had little faith that national policy makers, or even local elected officials, would act to protect their interests. The survey also indicated that the key to overcoming the reluctance of local populations to cooperate in light of perceived risk was local control and power sharing in siting and operation of the dumps. Financial inducements were less effective in encouraging cooperation.

Current Public Policy

There are currently three major national policy initiatives underway that are related to the problem of nuclear waste. The Waste Isolation Pilot Plant (WIPP), under construction in New Mexico, is a Department of Energy project that seeks to create a permanent repository for disposal of transuranic nuclear waste. State and regional programs are underway in response to the Low-Level Radioactive Waste Policy Act of 1980 (hereinafter Low-Level Waste Policy Act). This act made each state responsible for disposing of low-level radioactive waste generated within its borders (except for waste generated by defense or federal research and development activities). The Nuclear Waste Policy Act of 1982 (hereinafter Nuclear Waste Policy Act) established an elaborate process (later abandoned by act of Congress) for siting and development of two high-level nuclear waste repositories for commercially generated and defense waste.

A BRIEF HISTORY OF NUCLEAR WASTE POLICY

The history of public policy initiatives in the United States divides the subject of nuclear waste into two distinct spheres. Historically, the low-level waste problem has been managed by the creation of private, regional waste facilities licensed by the federal government. Access to these three waste facilities (located in South Carolina, Nevada, and Washington) has been restricted and is gradually being phased out by provisions of the Low-Level Waste Policy Act. Prior to this act, waste could be shipped to these facilities (for a disposal fee) from any state. Attempts by the sited states to restrict incoming waste were treated as unconstitutional restrictions of interstate commerce. However, this situation is changing in response to the demands of the sited states: federal policy has changed to make states accept responsibility for waste generated within their borders.

The high-level nuclear waste problem has had a more checkered history. In the 1960s the AEC considered various sites (including rock formations around the Savannah River nuclear facility and abandoned salt mines in Lyons, Kansas) as possible locations for high-level waste repositories. Local opposition and the strong possibility of environmental difficulties caused these sites to be abandoned. Without a satisfactory location for disposal of waste, a haphazard system of temporary storage evolved at nuclear facilities around the country. Often, these temporary storage facilities were unsound, resulting in contamination of some surrounding communities. The Nuclear Waste Policy Act sought to bring coherence to national policy for disposal of high-level nuclear waste.

The different ways in which the federal government has approached the problems of managing high- and low-level nuclear waste is instructive when considered from the regime perspective. Low-level waste policy has been implemented within a federalist regime that emphasizes state responsibility, interstate cooperation, and federal flexibility in cooperation with states. High-level waste policy had been implemented through a hybrid regime (bureaucratic with some federalist elements) that sought a technical solution to the problem of siting and designing a national facility with state consultation and veto power. Eventually, this process was abandoned. In the following sections, approaches to developing and implementing national policy that imposes costs are compared.

LOW-LEVEL NUCLEAR WASTE

The Nuclear Regulatory Commission has defined three categories of low-level nuclear waste: class A, B, and C (Yoder,

1987). Class A waste is characterized by low concentration levels of radionuclides, low curie levels, and quick decay rates. Class B waste is more radioactive than that in class A and is expected to be hazardous for approximately one hundred years. Class C waste consists of waste which requires as much as five hundred years to decay to an acceptable hazard level. Most of the volume of low-level nuclear waste is in class A. (Yoder [1987] reports a survey of the Midwest Compact, which indicates that 90 percent of its waste is class A, 9.5 percent class B, and .05 percent class C.) Although low-level waste is generally less hazardous than high-level waste, it remains a substantial threat to health and the environment and may require special packaging for transportation and disposal.

According to a DOE survey (reported by Furiga, 1989), the source and form of low-level nuclear waste is numerous. However, most of the volume of waste, some 51 percent when measured in cubic feet, is generated by utilities. This waste tends to be more potent than other sources since utilities account for more than 81 percent of all waste measured in curies. Other low-level waste is developed by industry, government, medical, and academic sources. In table 5, the results of the DOE survey of low-level nuclear waste for 1987 are reported.

Role of State Governments

Federal law governing the disposition of low-level nuclear waste requires that states devise legal compacts with other states to manage waste, or they must develop their own low-level nuclear waste facilities. Dan Berkovitz (1987) reports that this emphasis upon state responsibility reflects the state preferences first expressed by the State Planning Council on Radioactive Waste Management and later affirmed by the National Governors Association and the National Conference of State Legislatures (p. 443).

Though Congress enacted legislation that placed emphasis on state responsibility, it sought to encourage regional solutions to the low-level waste disposal problem. This may reflect the

TABLE 5
Low-Level Waste, 1987

Source	Cubic Feet (%)	Curies (%)
Utility	51.0	81.6
Industry	39.1	15.6
Government	7.1	2.6
Academic	1.6	—
Medical	1.2	—

Source: Reported in Yoder (1987).

belief that some states generate too little waste to operate waste facilities economically. However, the emphasis upon interstate cooperation created a substantial difficulty: How can federal policy formulators induce cooperation in the management of a politically unpopular problem such as nuclear waste?

A Federalist Regime

Federal low-level nuclear waste policy has encouraged regional solutions to nuclear waste management problems. The key to overcoming the reluctance of states to cooperate has been constitutional authority regarding interstate commerce. To induce regional cooperation, Congress has granted authority to compacting states (those who enter congressionally approved interstate compacts) to restrict waste accepted at their disposal site only to those generated by states within the compact. This license to interfere with interstate commerce is reserved for compacting states only. Those states who choose to go it alone are not permitted to restrict the importation of waste from other states. Berkovitz (1987) suggests that this has had the effect of causing larger waste producers to incorporate the service of smaller waste producers within their plans (p. 465).

Strategic Context

To understand the strategic context in which policy is implemented, consider the preferences and strategic options for states under the Low-Level Waste Policy Act. Each state is likely to evaluate the possible outcomes as follows. Given the political volatility of nuclear waste, the most desirable outcome for each state is to exploit others by sending their waste out of their jurisdiction for a fee. Following this, states are likely to prefer cooperation, sharing costs in a regional compact to operate a waste facility. Next, states are likely to favor policy stagnation—an uncoordinated exchange of problems in which states are free to export their waste but must also accept imports from others. But certainly, the least preferred outcome for each and every state is to be exploited—to have other states send waste to their jurisdiction while they are incapable of retaliating. These are the preferences of a Prisoner's Dilemma (see figure 17). Following the discussion in chapter 3, the obvious problem with such a strategic context is that the pursuit of self-interest by each state can lead to an outcome that all view as suboptimal.

The presentation above assumes that all states have equivalent preferences. However, important differences may emerge depending upon the amount of waste produced by a given state. If so, the strategic context may be even more confounding than Prisoner's Dilemma. States that produce large volumes of nuclear waste might actually prefer policy stagnation to cooperation. This is because relatively large producers would be likely to realize a net benefit in an unrestricted arrangement in which they could freely exchange problems with states that produce less waste. The greater volume of generated waste would give these states less incentive to cooperate with those who could retaliate only by sending small volumes of waste back at them. Thus, the strategic context is Deadlock because whenever one of the participants prefers mutual defection to mutual cooperation no incentive exists to cooperate. This is the likely position of states that produce large volumes of waste. Is there any hope of regional solutions and cooperation among states in this context?

In light of this, federal inducements to create interstate compacts must be quite powerful, and, in fact, they are. Consider the difference between a state that enjoys membership in a com-

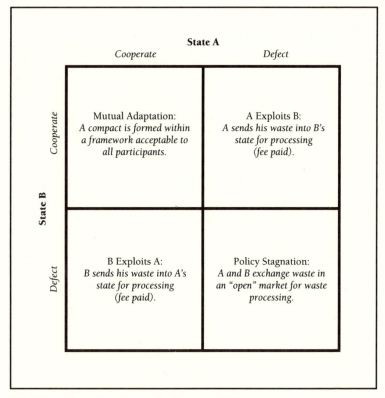

FIG. 17. Prisoner's Dilemma for Low-Level Waste

pact and one that does not. The compacted state enjoys the security of being insulated, by congressionally approved restraint
of interstate commerce, from the possibility that waste might be
sent in from a state outside its compact. To enjoy this protection, a state is required to select the compromise strategy in
which policy is implemented through mutual adaptation and
interstate cooperation. States that go it alone are subject to exploitation by all others—compacted and noncompacted states
—and can hope at best for the possibility of mutual exploitation
with other noncompacted states (who may also be large producers of waste). By precluding the possibility that small vol-

ume producers could be exploited by large ones Congress has created a strategic context in which even states that produce large volumes of waste are confronted with a powerful reason to compact with others in implementing a regional solution to the low-level nuclear waste problem.

Federal policy induces interstate cooperation by creating a strategic context in which those who do not cooperate are subject to exploitation by others. By rewarding cooperation through the compacting process, the federal government does not overcome the natural inclination of states to prefer to exploit others; rather, it creates an institutional mechanism that makes this possibility unlikely. States cooperate from enlightened self-interest, not from federal rules and requirements or monitoring of compliance.

The Limits of Federalist Regimes

The federalist character of the Low-Level Waste Policy Act gives states the necessary authority to make key decisions in response to federal demands that they accept responsibility for low-level waste. In doing so, the federal government's influence on such matters as where to locate and how to manage low-level waste sites is diminished. This is beneficial to the extent that policy decisions reflect local rationality; however, the evolution of policy may also reflect state politics at the expense of important technical considerations. Federalism does not guarantee policy improvement, but it does influence the political dynamics of the implementation process by shifting the locus of power to the state level.

Implementation Progress

To motivate timely state responses, Congress amended the Low-Level Waste Policy Act in 1985, adopting a series of intermediate deadlines (milestones) and requirements for licensing and site selection. States that do not comply with federal goals and timetables are subject to financial sanctions and may be restricted from transporting their waste across state lines to existing dumps. These incentives have induced most states to join a compact and move toward compliance with federal milestones. However, problems remain to be solved. Siting decisions continue to be controversial, deadlines have been pushed back, mounting costs are a concern, and some have questioned whether the federal government intended for so many regional sites to be developed (Furiga, 1989).

But in one important sense the Low-Level Waste Policy Act has been successful. It has motivated states to form compacts or establish their own plans for the creation of low-level nuclear waste repositories. Considering that the initial strategic context was Deadlock or Prisoner's Dilemma, this is an accomplishment. It is significant that the federal government has been able to engage states as partners in a circumstance in which each had said "Not in my backyard."

HIGH-LEVEL NUCLEAR WASTE

The hazardous nature and long life of high-level nuclear waste requires a repository that offers stable geology, an absence of ground water, and isolation from human populations for thousands of years. The dangers of handling and storing high-level nuclear waste dictate an elaborate waste disposal process. Currently, two sorts of waste processing facilities are being developed. A defense waste processing facility in Aiken, South Carolina, will prepare defense waste for storage in a permanent repository (perhaps encased in glass, see *The Washington Post,* 11/7/89, p. A3). A monitored retrievable storage system or MRS, such as that proposed for Oak Ridge, Tennessee, would serve as a site for temporary storage and consolidation of waste prior to shipment to a permanent repository.

The extent of federal responsibility for high-level nuclear waste depends upon its source: for waste generated by defense-related activities or federal research and development, the federal government has exclusive responsibility; for commercially generated waste, the Nuclear Waste Policy Act states that the federal government has a responsibility to protect public safety and safeguard the environment by assuring proper storage of radioactive waste. However, the act also notes that those responsible for generation of the waste should bear the costs of waste disposal and provide interim storage.

A Bureaucratic Regime (with Reservations)

To implement high-level waste management policy, the Nuclear Waste Policy Act created a hybrid regime by combining elements of the bureaucratic and federalist regime types (for a discussion of the general characteristics of these regime types, see chapter 4). There is inevitable tension between the centralizing forces of the bureaucratic regime and the shared public authority of the federalist regime. The bureaucratic regime downplays the importance of politics and participation and values central authority, information, and knowledge in order to find appropriate technical solutions to problems. The federalist regime views states as key partners in the development and implementation of national policy.

The mixed character of the regime may reflect the history of nuclear policy in the United States. The bureaucratic component of the regime—the value placed on technical expertise—reflects the early history of nuclear policy in which the federal government was dominant and state governments played a limited role by design. Perhaps this is a legacy of the postwar period when atomic technology was exotic and little understood. Members of the atomic subgovernment could argue forcefully for centralized authority on the grounds of national security and technical expertise.

The development of the atomic bomb was a testament to the capacity of the federal government's experts to manage the technology that military necessity had spawned. Only those who had developed atomic weapons could understand the risks and costs associated with this new technology. The public remained largely ignorant, depending upon the government's experts and trusting them to find safe and constructive uses for atomic energy. In this political climate, great value is placed upon technical expertise, and policy is developed and implemented through centralized mechanisms that offer limited opportunities for participation and popular control.

However, faith in the technical expertise and public interest orientation of the atomic subgovernment was short-lived. As people became more aware of the risks and hazards of nuclear technology, they became less accepting of expert opinion as the basis for making nuclear policy decisions. Scandalous incidents such as the release of nuclear materials into the atmosphere around the federal reservation in Hanford, Washington (Steele, 1988), or the lax standards for control of nuclear waste in Fernald, Ohio, and other locations (see *Time,* 10/31/88) indicated to the public the inability or unwillingness of technical experts to balance concern for the public interest with programmatic imperatives. Reflecting this more recent history and the perceived risk of nuclear technology, the siting process has incorporated federalist elements.

Implementing the Siting Process

The difficulties of implementing policy within a hybrid regime are evident from the federal government's frustrating attempts to locate sites for the nation's high-level waste repositories. Reflecting bureaucratic imperatives, the Nuclear Waste Policy Act states that the "geologic conditions" of potential sites are to be "the primary criteria" for selection. The secretary of the DOE was directed to undertake the selection process in several stages. In the first stage, the DOE was directed to screen potential sites and recommend to the president three from a list of five potential candidates for "characterization"—a process by which scientific and technical surveys would be performed to assess the suitability of the site as a long-term disposal facility. Concerns in the characterization process would include geological stability, ability to absorb heat, and potential for leeching of waste into the water table.

The act reserved the president's right to review the recommendations of the secretary of the DOE and accept or refuse the list of candidate sites. Upon completion of site characterization, the president was to recommend to Congress one of the three characterized sites as "qualified" for construction of the first repository.

Technical considerations notwithstanding, elements of the federalist regime also are present to counterbalance the technical rationality of the siting process. The Nuclear Waste Policy Act contained elaborate provisions for notification of and consultation with state governments (and tribal governments of native Americans, if appropriate). These provisions were designed to facilitate state and local participation and even went so far as to provide a state selected as the site of the high-level waste repository with veto power. When sites were accepted as candidates for characterization, the secretary of the DOE was to notify the state governments and provide grants to the states to facilitate participation in the decision-making process. The state recommended for siting the repository would retain the right to veto the selection, but this veto could be overridden by majority vote of both houses of Congress. (Congress wrote extensive requirements into the legislation to limit committee deliberation, floor debate, amendments, and parliamentary maneuvers when considering a "resolution of repository site approval.") If the state's "notice of disapproval" was not overridden by the Congress, the President was to select a second site as "qualified" within one year.

A second selection process, following the same basic process outlined above, but for areas in the eastern half of the United States—to achieve regional balance—was to follow the initial one. In 1986, this aspect of the selection process was suspended indefinitely in a move widely interpreted as a result of political considerations by the Reagan administration, including the desire not to upset the campaigns of Republican senatorial candidates whose states may have been under consideration. A GAO report (1987) indicates that states under consideration as sites for the first repository took the suspension of the search for the second site to mean that all of the nation's high-level nuclear waste would be placed in only one site.

In its attempt to execute the first stage of the process outlined above, the DOE recommended three possible sites to the president: Deaf Smith County, Texas, Hanford, Washington, and Yucca Mountain, Nevada. But it was not long before the siting process was abandoned.

The "Screw Nevada" Bill

In 1987, Congress reversed itself and suspended the site selection process that had been the centerpiece of the Nuclear Waste Policy Act. Of the three sites recommended by the DOE, only one was to be characterized: Yucca Mountain, Nevada. Sites in Texas and Washington were eliminated from further consideration. (Why these potential sites were eliminated is not clear, though political considerations loom large.) If the Yucca Mountain site is deemed unacceptable following the characterization process, the DOE must return to Congress for instructions.

Other changes in the 1987 legislation included postponement of the establishment of a monitored retrievable storage (MRS) facility, the abandonment of the second round of site selection, the creation of a special negotiator to work with states on selection problems, payment of ten million dollars per year to the host state (twenty million dollars while the site is being loaded) in exchange for waiving veto rights and accepting ineligibility for federal impact aid; and the establishment of an Office of Seabed Research (a new office to investigate the possibility of creating a waste repository in the subseabed).

The decision has been decried as foul play by officials from Nevada. Then-governor Richard Bryan issued a statement reprinted in *The Nevada Nuclear Waste Newsletter* (hereinafter *Newsletter*), February 1988: "In the bicentennial year of the Constitution, Congress gave a shameful demonstration of constitutional government. Forty nine states ganged up on Nevada and said they intend to locate the country's first high level nuclear waste dump at Yucca Mountain. Like sharks at a feeding frenzy, the states attacked Nevada."[1] Governor Bryan subsequently accused the DOE of suppressing a report that concluded that geological and hydrologic defects may exist at the Yucca Mountain site. The DOE claimed that the report had not been withheld from Congress and that it was a draft report that was not released pending peer review (*Newsletter*, 2/88).

Federalism at Its Worst?

Walter Rosenbaum (1987) argues that the site selection process authorized under the Nuclear Waste Policy Act was "federalism at its worst." By this he means to spread the blame for poor performance in the location and development of the waste repository to two sources. The federal government is culpable for its "bungling of earlier efforts to find an acceptable site," making states "suspicious about Washington's fairness and competence in the selection process." State governments are blamed for using powers at their disposal to frustrate federal attempts to solve the problem (p. 146)—from intervention by congressional delegations, as "one state after another maneuvered in Congress to ensure its exclusion from consideration," to use of state prerogatives to deny permits and other documents necessary for the DOE to complete its tasks.

Though the federalist element of the Nuclear Waste Policy Act was always tenuous—the state veto could be overridden by Congress—the changes in the site selection process indicate an abandonment of the values central to the initial search. No longer would even the technical criteria outlined in the act rule the day. Instead, Congress limited the options to a single site on the basis of preliminary, disputed data. Further consideration of alternative sites would occur only if this site was unsatisfactory—a far cry from bureaucratic rationality.

Echoing the disability thesis and reflecting the difficulties of imposing costs in a context of diffuse authority, Rosenbaum (1987) observes: "Resistance to designation among the states and numerous opportunities for political and legal obstruction have slowed the site selection process to a crabbed pace unlikely to achieve the act's mandated deadlines" (p. 147). Difficulties in the site selection process resulted from a clash between those who favored location of the site on the basis of technical criteria—implying a "preferred" solution can be defined by scientific means—and those who view the site selection process as essentially political—implying that position and representation are the most important determinants of the decision.

Bureaucracy at Its Worst?

The discussion of the bureaucratic regime in chapter 4 suggests that bureaucracy is not apolitical; rather, it may be a means to empower those who hold certain views or accept certain conditions as "necessary" for sound policy. The claim bureaucratic authority has to legitimacy is its "technical neutrality" in executing directives provided by public authority. Decisions made on the basis of technical criteria gain legitimacy and status as technically superior (at least in the limited sense of reflecting design criteria devised by public authority). Though the criteria are often imprecise and are themselves implicit value judgments, instrumental rationality is realized if they are responsibly applied by competent experts. Were the three sites recommended for characterization by the DOE selected on the basis of technical criteria?

One can debate whether the siting process conducted by the DOE was purely an application of technical criteria outlined by Congress. Karen Steele (1988) suggests that the elevation of the Hanford, Washington, site to one of the three recommended to the president for characterization may be an indication of a hidden agenda to locate a single site large enough to accommodate all of the nation's high-level waste (an imperative that contradicts the original site selection process outlined by Congress). Bitter residents and state officials from Nevada have speculated that the DOE favored the Yucca Mountain site principally because the federal government already owned property there. If so, bureaucratic politics, not bureaucratic rationality, may have affected the site selection process.

Strategic Context

The strategic context in which the high-level waste site selection process has been implemented is Deadlock. This is because the sited state would prefer policy stagnation to any other outcome. So long as this is true, federal policy makers can expect (as GAO reported, 1987) that states (and tribes of native Americans) affected by the siting decision will fight tooth and nail.

Consider the preferences of a state such as Nevada, now the most likely site for the repository. The most preferred outcome (by far) is that the repository will not be built on the proposed site, policy stagnation will occur requiring a new site or some other disposal method be found. Following this, the state would prefer to exploit the possibility that the site be built in their jurisdiction by receiving excessive compensation and control. Third, the state would prefer cooperation in which their concerns would be accommodated through consultation and participation. Finally, the state would least prefer compliance with the federal site selection process, whereby federal technicians, or their contractors, would site, develop, and operate the facility. There is no incentive to cooperate. As indicated in figure 18, the state's dominant strategy is to defect because resistance leads to the two most preferred outcomes.

Perhaps it is too optimistic to describe this strategic context as Deadlock. The preferences of the sited state indicate the impossibility of satisfaction through negotiation, regardless of the concessions offered. There are limits to the possibility of bargaining when one of the participants prefers stagnation even to agreement to dominate the process through exploitation. Whatever concessions are offered will be insufficient.

Federal preferences are the opposite. The federal government, given its apparent desire to consider only the Nevada site for characterization (perhaps to avoid further conflict and delay

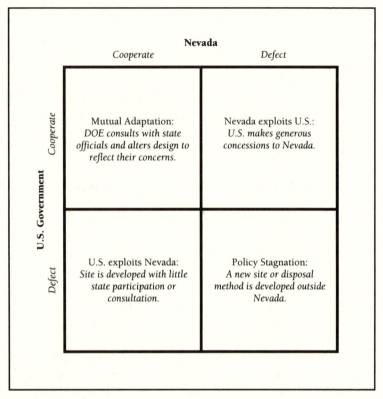

FIG. 18. Deadlock (at Best) in High-Level Waste

or to preclude serious consideration of other options), prefers compliance, cooperation, and exploitation or stagnation (the ordering of the last two is unclear). It is possible that federal policy makers would accept exploitation at the hands of the sited state if it meant getting the process moving. But, as the discussion of the state's preferences pointed out, even this may not be enough.

The federal policy initiative does nothing to account for the difficulties presented by this strategic context. Beyond this, the history of poor federal performance in protecting local concerns and the decision to abandon the original site selection process make it likely that the sited state will continue to use all means at its disposal to frustrate federal intentions.

Prospects for the Future

In November 1989, DOE Secretary James Watkins notified state leaders in Nevada that the state had thirty days to "decide to cooperate" or face a suit from the Justice Department. When the deadline for cooperation passed, the Bush administration sued the state of Nevada to allow work on assessing the suitability of the Yucca Mountain site for the high-level nuclear waste repository. The state leadership, especially Governor Robert Miller, had undertaken various legal and administrative means to block progress. For example, to frustrate federal scientists hoping to perform tests to determine the integrity of the site for long-term storage, the governor had refused to issue environmental permits required for the surveys (*The Washington Post,* 11/29/89, p. A2).

The federal government won a judgment against Nevada in the U.S. Circuit Court of Appeals to allow site characterization activities to continue. Nevada's attempts to block the characterization process were deemed to be premature as the Nuclear Waste Policy Act provided for a state veto only after the president recommended a characterized site to Congress as being qualified for construction of the repository (*The Washington Post,* 9/20/90, p. A17).

There are sound reasons to expect that the prospects for the future are bleak. No state is inclined to accept the site without resistance. The false starts and controversies in the siting process are likely to harden state opposition, especially since the state can point (with some justification) to fairness as a key issue. Resistance is likely to be especially spirited because the consequences of cooperation are unknown, but the costs and risks of cooperation are perceived to be long term and serious. The state that accepts the repository is placing its trust in the federal government (or its agents) to act responsibly to protect the state's interests for thousands of years to come. But federal officials have a historical record that does not create trust and goodwill. To the contrary, with the federal government's record concerning the health and environmental consequences of nuclear technology, it is little wonder that states fear that cooperation could become exploitation.

Federalism provides states with a variety of means to resist national policy initiatives. Given this, it is likely that the pattern of disputes will continue to be played out until all feasible options for state resistance are foreclosed. States can engage in a war of attrition and hope that the federal government will eventually be exhausted. In the meantime, they have nothing to lose.

LESSONS LEARNED:
THE IMPOSITION OF COSTS

Contrary to the disability thesis, diffuse authority does not preclude the possibility of implementing policy that imposes costs. However, the two policies examined in this chapter can be seen as distinct ways of approaching the problem of imposing costs. One approach is to motivate the acceptance of responsibility as federal low-level waste policy has done. The success of this initiative (though limited) is a result of the creation of a strategic and institutional context that has two essential elements. First, states do not benefit from policy stagnation. Second, cooperation among states is induced through the provision of constitutional authority that makes noncooperating states vulnerable to exploitation.

In comparison, federal attempts to site the nation's high-level waste repository show little concern for strategic or institutional context. The strategic context is Deadlock and no institutional mechanisms have been developed to overcome this difficulty. States benefit from policy stagnation and so have defected consistently.

Clearly, the siting process for a high-level waste repository has been unsuccessful; could it have been otherwise? The site selection process was ostensibly designed to find a technical solution (a site for locating the repository that was as safe and sound as possible). Given the nature of the problem of storing high-level nuclear waste, technical concerns are important and legitimate, but they are also complex (especially considering the need to anticipate what may happen thousands of years into the future). If there are multiple dimensions of concern in siting a repository, it is unlikely that any single site will emerge as the "best" location when uncertainty and honest differences about the weight of technical criteria are acknowledged. If this is so, it is inevitable that the decision will reflect concerns other than technical superiority (such as economy of construction and operation or minimization of political flak).

In his discussion of the high-level nuclear waste problem, Charles Montage (1987) presents an interesting parallel to the discussion of authority and exchange in chapter 2. He identifies two alternative strategies to design solutions: bureaucratic and market-oriented. The bureaucratic strategy (consistent with aspects of the initial siting process under the Nuclear Waste Policy Act) would identify clear, objective technical criteria for the siting and design of the facility and exclude, or at least seek to minimize, the influence of politics. The market-oriented approach would find several satisfactory sites (one presumes based upon technical criteria) and seek to induce cooperation by fostering competition between potential sites by offering an attractive package of financial inducements.

The most recent changes in high-level nuclear waste policy seem to reflect Montage's views. Though they have not selected several sites to create competition, policy formulators have offered financial compensation to the sited state in exchange for acceptance of the repository. Implicit in this approach is the belief that anything can be bought and that the real issue is price. However, consideration of the state's strategic position suggests that no level of financial compensation is likely to induce cooperation. Competition is irrelevant. Beyond this, if the research regarding low-level nuclear waste in Pennsylvania (Bord, 1987) can be extended to high-level waste in Nevada, financial inducements may be a poor substitute for local control and participation. If so, federal attempts to privatize the nuclear waste problem by buying cooperation are likely to be ineffective.

Uncertainty about the future and the limits of technical knowledge imply that a key to inducing cooperation is in assuring local populations that the repository won't be sited and forgotten. The federal commitment and local trust must span thousands of years. If there is no possibility of retreat, there is no shadow of the future, and once committed, local populations may be subject to exploitation by a federal government whose priorities and concerns focus elsewhere. The history of the nation's nuclear policy contains too many violations of trust to expect that citizens or political leaders will blindly accept federal willingness to protect their well-being. Only recognition and direct confrontation of these difficulties holds hope that the federal government can resolve the problem of locating sites for high-level nuclear waste repositories.

CONCLUSION

This chapter has compared two federal policies developed to dispose of nuclear waste. The low-level waste initiative placed emphasis upon state responsibility and made use of innovative constitutional authority to induce interstate cooperation. As a result, states are moving to implement federal requirements for low-level waste disposal. High-level waste policy has been less successful. While creating a hybrid regime that combined bureaucratic and federalist elements, federal policy failed to recognize or account for the strategic context in which policy was implemented. This, in conjunction with the mixed history of federal nuclear policy, has combined to create a context in which states benefit from obstruction and delay.

7   MEETING THE CHALLENGE

THE PROBLEMS of implementing national policy in the United States cannot be separated from the process of governing a liberal, federal polity. Liberalism and federalism divide control of policy-relevant resources. This diffusion of authority often challenges national leadership by introducing reluctant partners to the implementation process. To meet this challenge, the cooperation of implementors in pursuit of national policy goals must be gained. Cooperation does not require an absence of conflict; it is a response to conflict that may be influenced through attention to strategic and institutional context.

Established views of the implementation problem downplay the importance of cooperation, focusing instead upon the creation of comprehensive authority or the development of policy unlikely to create significant opposition. These views reflect the disability thesis—the belief that diffuse authority disables government. The implementation paradox emerges from this belief when national policy challenges those who control policy-relevant resources. In this way, the implementation process is seen as an Achilles's heel for U.S. government—the value of national policy initiatives is diminished by the incompetence or malice of the implementors.

In this work a revised view of the implementation process has been presented which focuses upon the design and development of implementation regimes. Based upon a distinctive conception of political power, power as the "capacity to act" (Stone, 1989), this view questions the claim that constitutional principles have disabled U.S. government. The implementation process need not constrain national power, but it may generate the power to achieve policy goals even in a condition of diffuse authority and conflict.

If the regime perspective has merit, diffuse authority need not be seen as a political arrangement in opposition to effectiveness. However, this does not imply that the U.S. government is functioning as well as could be expected. To improve national policy, more emphasis must be placed upon understanding and accounting for the strategic context in which implementation occurs and upon the development of effective mechanisms for inducing cooperation. This chapter traces the implications of regime analysis and suggests how national policy could be designed to better account for diffuse implementation authority.

IMPLICATIONS OF REGIME ANALYSIS

Several significant consequences are likely to result from viewing the implementation problem from the regime perspective. First, the nature of compound majorities and their effect upon national policy must be refined. Second, some of the conventional wisdom that has grown from implementation analysis must be reconsidered. Third, the evaluative content of implementation analysis is likely to become more dependent on context and arguable standards of performance. Finally, when considered from the regime perspective, the character of national policy itself is seen in a different light.

Compound Majorities

Vincent Ostrom (1987) has argued that a federal system of administration requires that national policy be supported by a series of majorities. This argument reflects the typical pattern of federal policy implementation in the United States in which some form of enabling legislation is required for state participation in federal programs. The initial majority of Congress must be compounded by majorities of the representatives within each state. In this way, states are a check on the power of the federal government as national policy initiatives are subject to a more strenuous test. However, Ostrom does not discuss the effect that federal programs may have upon the incentives of state representatives.

The creation of a federal program is likely to affect state politics and the dispositions of state representatives. Federal programs attract supporters and opponents at the state level who press their demands there, influencing the preferences of state authorities. It is possible that policy cliques within each state could use the creation of a federal policy initiative as a means of leveraging support from the state house regardless of the initial disposition of state representatives or the preferences of citizens excluded from the clique. It is also possible that the creation of a federal program could mobilize and galvanize opposition at the state level.

The ability of the federal government to induce cooperation is affected by its willingness to offer resources as part of its implementation plan. When a federal program offers resources to a state, the state representative may forego the opportunity offered by the program (and become vulnerable to the charge that an opportunity to "bring home the bacon" has been missed), or the representative may quiet the demands of the clique by agreeing to participate. The provision of resources is a powerful incentive for state representatives to follow the federal lead. If so, the decision to participate is not an independent assessment of the state's position on the issue, it is in part a reaction to the creation of national policy. This implies that there is potential for federalism to be undermined by an active national government (especially if it is flush with resources). Thus, while federalism may require the creation of compound majorities to implement national policy, these majorities are not constructed independently.

Similar political consequences are implied by the discussion of the National School Lunch Program and policy reform in chapter 5. In that case, the federal government was able to gain the cooperation of state authorities and responsiveness to changing federal priorities for several reasons: the implementation process was insulated from public scrutiny (Stone, 1980); the implementation regime had created an organization of policy professionals who sympathized with federal policy goals;[1] and the issue of changing priorities was not "politicized" because new authority for state officials to act was not required. The policy reform strategy described there should not be celebrated unconditionally for it is a means to circumvent diffuse authority and, as such, may be subject to abuse.

In the United States, the tendency to undermine federalism is mitigated somewhat by the active role states play in the development of national policy (recall, for example, the discussion of state participation in the development of low-level nuclear waste policy in chapter 6), the desire of national legislators to exceed constitutional requirements for state participation (as indicated by the discussion of Elazar's [1972] research in chapter 1), and the current budgetary climate in Washington. This implies that the national policy making process is likely to recognize the need for cooperation and generate policy that anticipates and accounts for state objections. Thus, no substantial changes in the policy-making process would be required to develop national policy that is consistent with the regime perspective.

Conventional Wisdom

The participation of numerous implementors is thought to create undue complexity in the implementation process, undermining performance (Pressman and Wildavsky, 1983). From the regime perspective, complexity is no longer viewed as a pure loss of implementation effectiveness. Complexity may be a consequence of other values that the implementation process must serve, such as representation of interest or protection from the possible abuses of centralized authority. Beyond this, expansion of the number of implementation participants may be part of a sound strategy to induce cooperation. Implementation analysts can contribute to efforts to improve national governance if they can distinguish complexity that is truly unnecessary from that which serves other key values or facilitates cooperation.

Implementation problems are most often seen as problems of hierarchical control, so it is common to suggest that new organizations are more likely than established ones to be responsive to political authority (see Downs, 1967, pp. 160–61; Pressman and Wildavsky, 1983, p. 128). The regime perspective qualifies this notion, suggesting that history and the shadow of the future are important to inducing cooperation. Established organizations, then, are more likely to be effective at inducing cooperation during the implementation process because they enjoy stability and a known reputation. If policy requires the cooperation of other authorities, a possible dilemma exists. If established organizations are more difficult for political authorities to control, the ability to control organizations varies inversely with organizational effectiveness in a context of diffuse authority (for an example of the possible problems faced by a new organization during the implementation process, see the discussion of the Economic Development Administration in chapter 3).

Subgovernments are often thought to dominate policy formulation and implementation, suggesting that existing organizational arrangements are key constraints upon policy improvement. The regime framework views existing organizational arrangements as resources (following the discussion in chapter 5, they are possible opportunities for reform). While existing organizations are forces to be reckoned with, the key is in constructing a strategic context in which implementation participants cannot benefit from obstruction and delay. Implementation analysts must determine how interorganizational relationships that are ripe for reform can be identified and what implications various regime design options have upon policy outputs.

Evaluating Implementation Performance

Evaluative standards are the basis for judging implementation performance. The regime perspective implies that criteria that are appropriate for judging implementation performance are more likely to be influenced by context. The standards that are appropriate for evaluating implementation performance are ambiguous because contradictory desires coexist—the process of governing must encourage patterns of cooperation guided by the national government while retaining a diffuse distribution of authority. Cooperation is not equivalent to compliance. However, cooperation must have purpose beyond the mere satisfaction of implementation participants. Regime analysis must highlight the connection between governing arrangements in the implementation process and the extent to which one value is emphasized over the other. The problem for implementation analysts is to discover which governing arrangements strike a proper balance between the competing values that the implementation process must serve.

The Character of National Policy

Thinking about implementation from the regime perspective also has implications for the character of national policy. First, the regime perspective reinforces the conventional view that national policy is a blunt instrument. The incomplete authority of policy formulators and the need to induce cooperation from others implies that policy must evolve during the implementation process. Federal policy makers would do well to abandon the illusion that they may define policy with surgical precision. Attempts to "program" the implementation process overlook changing circumstances or the possibilities for opportunistic behavior by implementors and lead to unwarranted faith in hierarchy and control.

Second, the scope of the implementation problem is more extensive than the implementation literature has acknowledged. The implementation process is political in the most basic sense—it is a reflection of constitutional principles at the core of U.S. government. If implementation is part of the governing process, the usual focus in the literature upon immediate programmatic objectives is far too narrow. Implementation analysis must account for the larger constitutional context in which federal programs operate and the larger purpose of governance which the implementation process serves. (The discussion in chapter 2 of Hayek's [1960] expansive view of the nature of policy is an important consideration for the implementation literature.)

LESSONS FOR POLICY DESIGN

Regime analysis has numerous implications for policy design. To make effective national policy, those who exercise political authority must be concerned with strategic and institutional context. Priority in policy design must be given to the incentive structure created by the initiative and the means by which cooperation may be induced during the implementation process. However, it is important to emphasize that the success of national policy depends upon the actions of all participants in the policy-making process. The need to induce cooperation implies the need for flexibility during implementation. Policy formulators alone cannot solve the problem. Though it is tempting to suggest that the lessons of regime analysis could be incorporated into the initial design of policy, thereby creating less need for discretion and flexibility during implementation (and rescuing overhead control), this is a false hope that belies the essence of the regime perspective—that implementation is part of the governing process and so is an arena in which policy must evolve to meet the legitimate concerns of participants.

Incentives and Strategic Context

Incentives are central to the regime perspective, though they are not seen as determinants of implementation behavior. The selection of participants identifies the incentives and strategic context of concern during the implementation process. Beyond this, participation empowers selected interests by placing them in a position to effect the evolution of policy. (The discussion in chapter 3 explains the relevance of strategic context, while chapter 4 clarifies the link between participation and power.) This implies that the selection of implementation participants is one of the most important decisions in policy design.

The regime perspective has a strong status quo bias. Effectiveness in a context of diffuse authority emphasizes that one must challenge, but also work with, existing authority. The federal government need not surrender to implementors, but must gain their cooperation. The discussion of strategic context in chapter 3 suggests that agreement on goals does not have to be extensive to induce cooperation (though certainly it is a convenient context in which to attempt to do so). What is required is that the strategic context offers a mixture of motives—some possibility for participants to gain—even though substantial compromise and oversight mechanisms may be required to avoid the temptation that participants have to exploit the process. If this is so, the importance of goal consensus (or lack of conflict) in the implementation process is generally overestimated. This implies that the purposes of federal policy are not limited merely to reflection of the desires of existing authority: the interests of implementors are considerations, not constraints, in policy design.

While it is true that participation is a form of empowerment, the power of position is limited. The link between position and power is tenuous if the purpose of participation is to redistribute power. When authority is diffuse, the need to create the capacity to act is likely to require that federal policy formulators select participants whose interests reflect and reinforce the existing distribution of power.[2] However, even for those who are selected to participate in the implementation process by virtue of their control of resources, the power of position is limited because it is shared. The primary power that comes from position, then, is defensive—it frustrates action by withholding cooperation. This makes the regime perspective's emphasis on inducing cooperation even more salient.

The discussion of low-level nuclear waste policy illustrated another key aspect of the selection of implementors—the assignment of responsibility. Diffuse authority was not an obstacle to progress in that case because a strategic and institutional context was created in which states were made to accept responsibility to respond to a festering public problem. This suggests that the tendency to view national problems as requiring national solutions may be counterproductive (Ostrom, 1987). If so, federal authorities must carefully consider at what level it is most appropriate to assign responsibility for resolving public problems.

In determining the level at which problems should be attacked, the strategic position of those who accept responsibility is a key consideration. The success of the low-level waste policy did not result merely from the assignment of responsibility to the state level, it emerged from the strategic context created by the federal government in doing so. Other policy domains may require different solutions. Federal policy formulators ought to resist the impulse to assign responsibility to the federal government by default, but they must also resist the impulse to abdicate responsibility.

Institutional Context

Aspects of institutional context can be planned in advance through effective policy design, but there are limits in the ability of policy formulators to anticipate problems and design solutions. One way that policy design can contribute to the creation of an effective institutional context is by building upon established partnerships. However, the limits of rationality imply that this matter should not be the exclusive province of policy for-

mulators. Implementors are naturally inclined to seek partnerships with those who control key resources and with whom they
enjoy an established history of constructive cooperation. In this
way, design limits can be overcome through regime development during the implementation process.

The possibility of policy reform also is an important consideration. Reform initiatives are by definition undertaken in a
context in which an established history and policy implementation process exists. While there may be a need for a change
of emphasis, the capacity of the existing implementing system
is a formidable resource.

Institutional means to induce cooperation may be developed
during implementation through attention to process, oversight,
and information sharing. The regime perspective implies that
the scope and vigor of oversight is much more important than
the incentive structure created by penalties (the more common
focus for concern). With the exception of the bureaucratic regime, the purpose of oversight during implementation is not to
control behavior with strict rules or to enforce sanctions that
outweigh the benefits of exploitation, but to encourage cooperation by assuring participants that those who exploit the process will be detected. This suggests that evaluation of outcomes
(when possible and appropriate) or transparency of process (if
outcomes cannot be evaluated) are important means to induce
cooperation.[3] Emphasis should be placed upon comprehensive,
though cursory, reviews of performance that initially screen and
detect possible exploitive behavior. Those suspected of exploitation could be targeted for further investigation and possible
sanctions. This procedure helps to mitigate the problems of
punishing "saints and sinners alike" (Gromley, 1989, p. 184).

The effectiveness of establishing standards of conduct should
not be underestimated when seeking to induce cooperation.
Perhaps it is natural to focus upon the dark side of administrative oversight—detection and punishment of deviant behavior—in the creation of administrative mechanisms. However,
the effect of what William Gromley (1989) has called "hortatory
controls" should not be overlooked. Cooperation is encouraged

by defining appropriate behavior and exhorting implementation participants to adopt positive models of behavior. This is the positive side of oversight which presumes that implementors are interested in constructive cooperation, but benefit from guidance about how to achieve it.

LESSONS FOR LEADERSHIP

A society that values diffuse authority places unusual demands upon its leadership. Political leaders are held accountable for aspects of life that are inconsistent with the scope of their authority. When responsibility does not correspond to control of resources, the purpose of political leadership is not to control behavior but to articulate the public's interest and create a context in which those who serve it benefit. Federal leaders must work in concert with other organizations and institutions to accomplish this. However, too often political leaders (and those who advise them) view lack of control and its source—diffuse authority—as the essential problem. Consequently, they degenerate into counterproductive attempts to design airtight systems of authority for implementing policy. Constructive leadership emphasizes the creation of a context for cooperation to accomplish public goals, not control.

The regime perspective also places great demands upon leadership in the implementation process. By recognizing the importance of policy evolution and the flexibility required to induce cooperation, implementors are given discretion to make key decisions. Leaders in the implementation process must concern themselves with generating responsible and effective means of coordinating the actions of participants they cannot control. Constructive leadership during implementation will create the means to coordinate activity without allowing those who cooperate to be exploited.[4]

In spite of formidable difficulties, there is cause for optimism. Contrary to the disability thesis, diffuse authority is not the enemy of public effectiveness. More importantly, consolidation of public authority is no panacea for the design and implementation of effective national policy. Those who value liberalism and federalism need not despair—through cooperation it is possible to govern while maintaining a diffusion of authority. If so, there is hope that the enduring challenge of U.S. government can be met.

Notes

Bibliography

Index

NOTES

1. The Implementation Paradox

1. The term *positive* is not meant to imply that the purposes of government are "good," but only that government seeks to use society's resources to accomplish some policy objective which otherwise would be unlikely to occur.

2. The term *constitutional* here should not be taken to imply that commercial organization is explicitly addressed in the text of the Constitution of the United States. Rather, it implies that this is a basic principle upon which key social institutions have been constructed in the United States.

3. Richard Nelson (1977) has argued that the contradiction between the static model that supports claims of market efficiency and the need for a dynamic change to support market innovation has not been resolved. See *The Moon and the Ghetto,* chap. 8, for a discussion.

4. One possibility is to create distinct spheres of authority: "dual federalism" and a strict separation of the public and private sectors would be the guiding principles of such an arrangement. However, dual federalism is compromised by the interaction policy issues; if policy cannot be carved neatly into separate spheres, neither can authority to make policy be so neatly divided. And the distinction between public and private authority quickly becomes ambiguous when the role of public authority in creating "private" authority is recognized (on this see Lindblom, 1977; Bozeman, 1987). A second possibility is the uncoordinated interaction of authorities. However, this begs the question of how competing authorities are constituted and twists the notion of organizing principles by making anarchy a blueprint for national governance.

5. Pressman and Wildavsky's (1983) analysis of the complexity of joint action is an example of how additional implementation partici-

pants might diminish the capacity of the federal government to act, even if they are willing partners. For a critique of their analysis, see Bowen (1982).

2. Authority, Exchange, and Governance

1. Many readers may be familiar with the distinction usually drawn in the literature between top-down and bottom-up approaches. I have deliberately avoided this distinction as a basis for organizing this presentation. It is true that the top-down approach typically associates government with authority and views implementation as a problem of organization—devising effective means to accomplish an agreed upon purpose. Hence, top-down analysis is quite consistent with Lindblom's authority paradigm. However, in my view, the contents of the authority paradigm also would include some portion of the bottom-up literature. Bottom-up analysts who assume that diffuse authority is illegitimate are in this category.

Diffuse authority and strategic behavior may be viewed as a means to exploit the implementation process—"problems" to be solved. This perspective is inconsistent with the exchange paradigm because it views exchange as a one-sided proposition: compromise and accommodation during the implementation process are seen as acts that reduce the ability of the federal government to achieve its objectives. Contrary to Lindblom's definition of exchange, which reflects the usual assumption that both parties benefit from this sort of relationship, this view suggests that exchange diminishes federal power or limits the scope and effectiveness of national policy options.

2. To some analysts (for example, Bardach, 1980), the problems are so profound that the agenda of the public sector should be limited.

3. Of course, those who view implementation from the bottom-up are likely to emphasize the importance of those "street level bureaucrats" who are the contact point between citizen and government (on this see Lipsky, 1980).

4. The term *objective* is defined broadly in this context to include both the ostensible purposes of the policy and the demands made by federal policy formulators for changes in the routines or behaviors of implementation participants.

5. Emmette Redford (1969, p. 41) discusses overhead democracy as a possible means to achieve democracy in administrative decision

making. From this perspective, democracy is infused into the process when "voter's representatives in legislative and executive positions . . . direct and control administrative organizations." Further discussion of overhead democracy can be found in Kenneth Meier, *Politics and the Bureaucracy,* 1979. This position is most clearly described in the implementation literature as Frank Thompson's (1984) concept of "controlled implementation."

6. As noted earlier, Bardach (1980) is an exception. His emphasis upon a fixer implies lack of faith in comprehensive policy design. However, he does imply that the fixer is capable of designing solutions to problems as they occur within the implementation process.

7. This makes bottom-up interpretations of the implementation problem consistent with public choice approaches to policy analysis and establishes a foundation for neoconservative critiques of federal leadership.

8. McLaughlin's (1976) views are also compatible with professionalism. The importance of professionalism in the successful implementation of federal programs was discussed by Peterson, Rabe, and Wong, 1986.

9. Depending upon the specific structure of the preferences, several different types of mixed motive interactions could exist. For a discussion of the different types, see Oye, 1985.

10. This view of political leadership is consistent with Talcott Parson's discussion of the role of leadership in the generation of political power. See Parsons, 1969, chap. 14.

3. Implementation Regimes

1. On the institutionalization of values, see Elkin, 1986; Selznick, 1957. The topic of political values in implementation regimes is developed in the following chapter.

2. Although the disciplinary subdivisions of political science would seem to belie it, an analogy exists between the problems of organizing cooperation in the international community and the problems of governing a federal polity, especially one with a liberal political economy. The problems are similar in that no single authority dominates the implementation of policy; a diffuse distribution of authority with the expectation of conflict among interested parties is characteristic. Although international analysts may view domestic governance

as less difficult for its limited violence, enforcement of property rights and contracts, and constitutional structure, the perceived ease of national governance is based in part upon the myth of automatic implementation. Domestic implementation shares an essential characteristic with international politics: the need to manage conflict and cooperation in a context of diffuse authority to accomplish policy goals.

3. In describing these conditions and subsequent games, the notational conventions of Oye (1985) are used. In each case the presentation is a pair of strategic choices—cooperation indicated by "C" and defection by "D." The pair is presented so that the choice of the party whose preferences are being described is first. For example, "CD" would indicate a circumstance in which a participant experienced unrequited cooperation.

4. To normalize the payoffs for each participant, set the lowest utility value equal to zero, then divide each value (expressed on an interval scale) by the highest value in the set. This makes the maximum payoff for each participant 1.0 and expresses all other values as a portion of this unit.

5. This conclusion is questioned by Elinor Ostrom in her 1989 paper.

6. It is important to acknowledge the possibility that public discourse might change the perspective of implementation participants to make them more aware of the consequences of their actions for others.

7. Lawrence Brown (1983) has discussed this possibility and the distinction between "rationalizing" politics and "breakthrough" politics. He has suggested that in rationalizing politics government may have more will to confront the iron triangles that dominate policy formulation (p. 45).

4. The Politics of Implementation Regimes

1. In hedging my bet, I am merely reflecting on the fact that the problem of tax compliance in the cash economy is so profound that it may be impossible to reliably estimate its scope.

2. Regulation is not always conflictual in the sense that commercial enterprises are always bound to resist it. Recently, apple growers requested the federal government to regulate the use of Alar in their industry. Apple sales had plummeted in response to growing public

concern about the use of this possible carcinogen. Regulation is a way for the industry to regain the public's confidence that apples are safe to eat.

3. Of course, this assumption is not always justified. Sometimes the implementation of a standard solution will be inappropriate or contribute to other problems. An example is the use of tall smoke-stacks in the Midwest to disperse airborne pollutants in communities where industry is concentrated. This solution improved air quality in the area surrounding the industry, but transported pollutants to the Northeast where they reappeared as acid rain.

4. The details of this illustration are drawn from an article in the *Washington Post* (6/21/89), "Legal Pollution That Makes Students Sick," by Michael Weisskopf, p. A1.

5. The term *shadow government* was used to describe the devel-opment policy process in a series of articles by the *Baltimore Sun* (see, for example, 4/13/80, p. A1).

6. The new emphasis is upon commercial development. See the *Baltimore Sun,* 4/31/86, p. D1.

7. Avoiding the pathos of bureaucracy by mimicking the market is a strategy for improving federal policy that predates the privatization movement. Alice Rivlin implied similar themes in her 1971 work, *Systematic Thinking for Social Action:*

> A new approach is in order: State the accountability in terms of outputs, and reward those who produce more efficiently. Free to vary the way they spend their money as long as they accomplish specified results, recipients of federal grants could be rewarded for producing beyond expectations. This procedure would liber-ate them from the straightjacket of input controls and promote vigorous and imaginative attempts to improve results, just as in large corporations plant managers are free to vary production methods, but rewarded and promoted according to sales and profits. . . . Even in programs run by the federal government it-self, productivity could be increased by allowing individual pro-ject managers—federal hospital administrators or training center heads, for example—more freedom and more incentive to achievement. (P. 127)

Rivlin asserts that flexibility, incentives, and competition are val-ues that can improve performance regardless of whether federal policy is implemented directly by federal agents, through intergovernmental arrangements, or through grants to third parties. The early implementation literature reflected this same emphasis when it offered the slogan "Payment on Performance" (Pressman and Wildavsky, 1983, p. 159). Since then, to suggest that the quality of public policy could be improved by mimicking the market has become orthodoxy.

8. Expanding this point, a parallel may be drawn to the discussion of regime development in chapter 3. There I argue that, over time, the development of the implementation regime makes cooperation more likely as participants become accustomed to dealing with one another and develop mutual expectations. Thus, the relationship that exists between participants in the regime undermines competition since those who do not have a history of cooperation are deemed less trustworthy. If the value of privatization depends upon market competition, the process of regime development undermines the value of privatization.

5. Policy Reform and Implementation Performance

1. This provision was dropped with program changes enacted under authority of the Omnibus Budget Reconciliation Act of 1981.

2. This authority was restricted by the 1981 budget act.

3. This was the conclusion of a report to the Senate Select Committee on Nutrition and Human Needs, January 1972. The report found that from 1947 to 1960, NSLP participation increased 250 percent while federal funding increased only 35 percent.

4. The growth in participation in this category was in part a consequence of the liberalization of eligibility standards as mandated by the Congress. Equally important, however, is the fact that this growth occurred within a context of overall increases in NSLP participation.

5. With the development of a federal Department of Education, HEW was reorganized as the Department of Health and Human Services (HHS).

6. HEW report, "Ten State Nutritional Survey," 1972.

7. GAO report, "The National School Lunch Program—Is It Working?," 1977, p. 38.

8. "Semi-Annual Report: Office of the Inspector General," USDA, October 1, 1978 to March 31, 1979.

9. See U.S. Senate, *Report to the Committee on the Budget*, 97th

Cong., 1st sess., #97-139, pp. 77–78. Of course, this is an overesti-
mate of the likely "savings" from reform initiatives, for it presumes
that all program applications that are invalid are resulting in undue
expense. A more likely result from reform is lower error rates with
little cost savings.

10. *New York Times,* 1/5/82, p. A1.

11. This test is executed in two stages. In the first stage, a tentative
model is estimated and diagnosed. The tentative ARIMA model describes the time series as noise (as a series that has patterned, but
irrelevant, variation over time). Once the tentative model has been
identified, intervention terms corresponding to changing federal priorities (triggered by dummy variables) are introduced. By discerning the
statistical significance of the parameters for the intervention term, conclusions may be drawn regarding the existence of a substantial discontinuity in the time series. If the intervention parameters are found
to be significant, this would be evidence that changes in implementation performance had occurred in the periods specified.

The location of intervention points (the point at which the dummy
variable representing program reform in the analysis is triggered) is a
point of ambiguity in this research. There is no reason to presume a
single intervention point, for this is tantamount to assuming that all
indicators in all states respond to the policy reform with identical dis-
patch. When policy change is complex, and its purpose is to induce
states to alter their performance, variation in the intervention point
should be expected. This makes identification (in advance) of a specific point at which program performance should change difficult. The
plausibility of the claim that changes in performance are due to intervention can be judged on two factors: How close to the actual reform do the changes occur? Is there a pattern of change in several
indicators of program performance?

12. Unless otherwise noted, results reported here are statistically
significant at least at the 95 percent level of confidence.

13. It is important be aware of the limits of intervention analysis.
The purpose of such analysis is to detect deviations from an underlying
pattern in the data and to determine whether these observed deviations
are of sufficient magnitude to be deemed statistically significant. The
proportion of free and reduced price lunches provided is an interesting
example of the limits of such analysis. The pattern of explosive growth
in free and reduced participation in the late 1960s is clear from the
plotted data. However, because the intervention model seeks a dis-

continuity in an underlying trend, no statistically significant effect of
intervention is found. This is because the explosive growth can be
neatly modeled as a first order autoregressive process; this captures
the discontinuity that is apparent to the eye in a parsimonious model.
The clear deviation from the early pattern (flat or declining free and
reduced participation rates) thus is absorbed into a larger pattern of
exponential growth. My interpretation, in spite of what my computer
output tells me, is that there is clear evidence of changes in program
performance in the late 1960s and that the pattern of change is consistent with the attempts by the federal government to assert the goal
of child nutrition, especially for the needy.

14. The patterns of change are even more striking when the data
are organized at the state level. Preliminary analysis of these data is
wholly consistent with the conclusions presented here.

6. Not in My Backyard

1. The often ironic relationship between federal policy makers and
their opponents is well illustrated by *The Nevada Nuclear Waste Newsletter*. This publication has been a forum for those in Nevada who have
sought to question the wisdom of the federal government's decision
to survey the site of Yucca Mountain for possible qualification as a
high-level nuclear waste repository. Of course, the newsletter—a publication of the Nevada Nuclear Waste Project Office—is underwritten
by a federal grant from the United States Department of Energy.

7. Meeting the Challenge

1. Peterson, Rabe, and Wong (1986) have discussed the tendency
for established programs to enjoy the support of a group of policy
professionals who value the program and share its goals.

2. The notable exception to this rule is the pluralist regime,
though its effect is highly uncertain and depends upon individual or
group initiative. When position is combined with control of resources,
empowerment is greatest. Federal policy may attempt to create "balance" in the implementation process by combining position with resources. An illustration of this was the provision of federal funds to
those opposed to federal nuclear waste policy in Nevada in chapter 6.

3. Donahue (1989) presents a discussion of the circumstances in which one might choose to focus upon outcome or process.

4. Donahue (1989) has argued that concern for exploitation is essential to an effective social order: "A culture's capacity to get things done depends greatly upon the quality of institutions it develops to allow people to delegate tasks to others, or to undertake them for others, without fear of exploitation" (p. 39).

BIBLIOGRAPHY

Allison, G. 1971. *Essence of Decision.* Boston: Little, Brown and Co.

Axelrod, R. 1984. *The Evolution of Cooperation.* New York: Basic Books.

————. 1970. *Conflict of Interest.* Chicago: Markham Publishing Co.

Axelrod, R., and R. Keohane. 1985. "Achieving Cooperation Under Anarchy: Strategies and Institutions." *World Politics* 39 (1): 226–54.

Bardach, E. 1980. *The Implementation Game.* Cambridge, Mass.: MIT Press.

Barrett, S., and M. Hill 1984. "Policy, Bargaining and Structure in Implementation Theory." *Policy and Politics* 12 (3): 219–40.

Baum, L. 1984. "Legislatures, Courts, and the Dispositions of Policy Implementors." In *Public Policy Implementation,* ed. G. Edwards, pp. 29–57. Greenwich, Conn.: JAI Press.

Benda, P., and C. Levine. 1988. "Reagan and the Bureaucracy: The Bequest, the Promise, and the Legacy." In *The Reagan Legacy: Promise and Performance,* ed. C. Jones, pp. 102–42. Chatham, N.J.: Chatham House Publishers.

Berkovitz, D. 1987. "Waste Wars: Did Congress 'Nuke' State Sovereignty in the Low-Level Radioactive Waste Policy Amendments Act of 1985?" *Harvard Environmental Law Review* 11 (2): 437–90.

Berman, P. 1980. "Thinking About Programmed and Adaptive Implementation: Matching Strategies to Situations." In *Why Policies Succeed or Fail,* ed. H. Ingram and D. Mann, pp. 205–27. Beverly Hills, Calif.: Sage.

————. 1978. "The Study of Macro- and Micro-Implementation." *Public Policy* 26 (2): 157–84.

Bord, R. 1987. "Judgements of Policies Designed to Elicit Local Cooperation on LLRW Disposal Siting: Comparing the Public and Decision Makers." *Nuclear and Chemical Waste Management* 7 (2): 99–105.

Bowen, E. 1982. "The Pressman-Wildavsky Paradox: Four Addenda on Why Models Based on Probability Theory Can Predict Implementation Success and Suggest Useful Tactical Advice for Implementors." *Journal of Public Policy* 2 (1): 1–21.

Bozeman, B. 1987. *All Organizations Are Public: Bridging Public and Private Organization Theories.* San Francisco: Jossey-Bass Inc.

Brown, L. 1983. *New Policies, New Politics: Government's Response to Government's Growth.* Washington, D.C.: Brookings.

Browne, A., and A. Wildavsky. 1983. "Implementation as Mutual Adaptation." In *Implementation,* 3rd ed., ed. J. Pressman and A. Wildavsky, pp. 206–31. Berkeley and Los Angeles: University of California Press.

Burnham, W., and M. Weinberg, eds. 1978. *American Politics and Public Policy.* Cambridge, Mass.: MIT Press.

Cook, T., and D. Campbell. 1979. *Quasi-Experimentation: Design and Analysis Issues for Field Settings.* Boston: Houghton Mifflin Co.

Department of Agriculture. 1979. "Semi-Annual Report: Office of the Inspector General." (1 October 1978–31 March 1979).

Derthick, M. 1972. *New Towns In-Town.* Washington, D.C.: Urban Institute Press.

Donahue, J. 1989. *The Privatization Decision: Public Ends, Private Means.* New York: Basic Books.

Downs, A. 1967. *Inside Bureaucracy.* Boston: Little, Brown, and Co.

Dresang, D., and J. Gosling. 1989. *Politics, Policy, and Management in the American States.* New York: Longman.

Edner, S. 1976. "Intergovernmental Policy Development: The Importance of Problem Definition." In *Public Policy Making in a Federal System,* ed. C. Jones and R. Thomas, pp. 149–67. Beverly Hills, Calif.: Sage Publications.

Edwards, G., ed. 1980. *Implementing Public Policy.* Washington, D.C.: Congressional Quarterly Press.

———. 1984. *Public Policy Implementation.* Greenwich, Conn.: JAI Press.

Elazar, D. 1987. *Exploring Federalism.* Tuscaloosa, Ala.: University of Alabama Press.

———. 1972. *American Federalism: A View from the States.* New York: Thomas Crowell Co.

Elkin, S. 1986. "Regulation and Regime: a Comparative Analysis." *Journal of Public Policy* 6 (1): 49–71.

Elmore, R. 1985. "Forward and Backward Mapping: Reversible Logic in the Analysis of Public Policy." In *Policy Implementation in Federal and Unitary Systems,* ed. K. Hanf and T. Toonen, pp. 33–70. Boston: Martinus Nijhoff Publishers.

————. 1982. "Backward Mapping: Implementation Research and Policy Decisions." In *Studying Implementation,* ed. W. Williams, pp. 18–35. Chatham, N.J.: Chatham House.

————. 1978. "Organizational Models of Social Program Implementation." *Public Policy* 26 (2): 185–228.

Etzioni, A. 1975. *A Comparative Analysis of Complex Organizations.* New York: The Free Press.

Furiga, P. 1989. "Hot Stuff." *Governing* 3 (November 1989): 50–57.

General Accounting Office. 1987. "Nuclear Waste: Institutional Relations Under the Nuclear Waste Policy Act of 1982." Washington, D.C.: Government Printing Office.

————. 1977. "The National School Lunch Program—Is It Working?" Washington, D.C.: Government Printing Office.

Goggin, M. 1986. "The 'Two Few Cases/Too Many Variables' Problem in Implementation Research." *Western Politics Quarterly* 39 (2): 328–47.

Golembiewski, R., and F. Gibson, eds. 1983. *Readings in Public Administration.* 4th ed. Boston: Houghton Mifflin Company.

Goodnow, F. 1967. *Politics and Administration.* New York: Russell and Russell.

Gromley, W. 1989. *Taming the Bureaucracy: Muscles, Prayers, and Other Strategies.* Princeton, N.J.: Princeton University Press.

Hanf, K., and T. Toonen, eds. 1985. *Policy Implementation in Federal and Unitary Systems.* Boston: Martinus Nijhoff Publishers.

Hardin, G. 1977. "The Tragedy of the Commons." In *The Tragedy of the Commons,* ed. G. Hardin and J. Baden, pp. 16–30. San Francisco: Freeman and Co.

Hardin, G., and J. Baden, eds. 1977. *The Tragedy of the Commons.* San Francisco: Freeman and Co.

Hayek, F. A. 1960. *The Constitution of Liberty.* Chicago: University of Chicago Press.

————. 1967. *Studies in Philosophy, Politics and Economics.* Chicago: University of Chicago Press.

Health, Education, and Welfare, Department of. 1972. "Ten State Nutritional Survey." Washington, D.C.: Government Printing Office.

Henig, J. 1985. *Public Policy and Federalism.* New York: St. Martin's Press.

Hiskes, A., and R. Hiskes. 1986. *Science, Technology, and Policy Decisions.* Boulder, Colo.: Westview Press.

Hirschman, A. 1970. *Exit, Voice, and Loyalty.* Cambridge, Mass.: Harvard University Press.

House of Representatives, Committee on Government Operations. 1980. "Automobile Fuel Economy: EPA Oversight." Washington, D.C.: Government Printing Office.

Ingram, H. 1977. "Policy Implementation through Bargaining." *Public Policy* 25 (4): 499–526.

Ingram H., and D. Mann, eds. 1980. *Why Policies Succeed or Fail.* Beverly Hills, Calif.: Sage Publications.

Jones, C., ed. 1988. *The Reagan Legacy: Promise and Performance.* Chatham, N.J.: Chatham House Publishers.

Jones, C., and R. Thomas. 1976. *Public Policy Making in a Federal System.* Beverly Hills, Calif.: Sage Publications.

Kettl, D. 1988. *Government by Proxy: (Mis?) Managing Federal Programs.* Washington, D.C.: Congressional Quarterly Press.

Keohane, R. 1984. *After Hegemony: Cooperation and Discord in the World Political Economy.* Princeton, N.J.: Princeton University Press.

Krist, M., and R. Jung. 1982. "The Utility of a Longitudinal Approach in Assessing Implementation: A Thirteen-Year View of Title 1, ESEA." In *Studying Implementation,* ed. W. Williams, pp. 119–48. Chatham, N.J.: Chatham House.

Lester, J., A. Bowman, M. Goggin, and L. O'Toole. 1987. "Public Policy Implementation: Evolution of the Field and Agenda for Future Research." *Policy Studies Review* 7 (1): 200–16.

Lindblom, C. 1977. *Politics and Markets.* New York: Basic Books.

Linder, S., and B. Guy Peters. 1987. "A Design Perspective on Policy Implementation: The Fallacies of Misplaced Prescription." *Policy Studies Review* 6 (3): 459–75.

Lipsky, M. 1980. *Street-level Bureaucracy: Dilemmas of the Individual in Public Services.* New York: Russell Sage Foundation.

McLaughlin, M. 1976. "Implementation as Mutual Adaptation: Matching Strategies to Situations." In *Social Program Implementation,* ed. W. Williams and R. Elmore, pp. 205–27. New York: Academic Press.

Majone, G., and A. Wildavsky. 1983. "Implementation as Evolution." In *Implementation,* 3rd ed., ed. J. Pressman and A. Wildavsky, pp. 163–80. Berkeley and Los Angeles: University of California Press.

Mazmanian, D., and P. Sabatier. 1983. *Implementation and Public Policy.* Chicago: Scott Foresman and Co.

Mazmanian, D., and P. Sabatier, eds. 1981. *Effective Policy Implementation.* Lexington, Mass.: Lexington Books.

Meier, K. 1979. *Politics and the Bureaucracy: Policymaking in the Fourth Branch of Government.* North Scituate, Mass.: Duxbury Press.

Mitnick, B., and R. Backoff. 1984. "The Incentive Relation in Implementation." In *Public Policy Implementation,* ed. G. Edwards, pp. 59–122. Greenwich, Conn.: JAI Press.

Montage, C. 1987. "Federal Nuclear Waste Disposal Policy." *Natural Resources Journal* 27 (Spring): 309–408.

Montjoy, R., and L. O'Toole. 1979. "Toward a Theory of Policy Implementation: An Organizational Perspective." *Public Administration Review* 34 (5): 465–76.

Nakamura, R., and D. Pinderhughes. 1981. "Changing Anacostia: Definition and Implementation." In *Implementing Public Policy,* ed. D. Palumbo and M. Harder, pp. 3–17. Lexington, Mass.: Lexington Books.

Nakamura, R., and F. Smallwood. 1980. *The Politics of Policy Implementation.* New York: St. Martin's Press.

Nigro, F., and L. Nigro, eds. 1983. *Readings in Public Administration.* New York: Harper & Row.

Nelson, R. 1977. *The Moon and the Ghetto.* New York: Norton and Co.

Olson, M. 1971. *The Logic of Collective Action.* Cambridge, Mass.: Harvard University Press.

Ostrom, E. 1989. "A Political Scientist's View of Policy Studies: Reflections on the Commons." Paper presented at the annual meeting of the American Political Science Association, Atlanta, August.

Ostrom, V. 1987. *The Political Theory of a Compound Republic.* Lincoln, Neb.: University of Nebraska Press.

O'Toole, L., and R. Montjoy. 1984. "Interorganizational Policy Implementation: A Theoretical Perspective." *Public Administration Review* 44 (6): 491–503.

Oye, K. 1985. "Explaining Cooperation Under Anarchy: Hypotheses and Strategies." *World Politics* 39 (1): 1–24.

Palumbo, D., and M. Harder, eds. 1981. *Implementing Public Policy.* Lexington, Mass.: Lexington Books.

Parsons, T. 1969. *Politics and Social Structure.* New York: The Free Press.

Peterson, P. 1981. *City Limits.* Chicago: University of Chicago Press.

Peterson, P., B. Rabe, and K. Wong. 1986. *When Federalism Works.* Washington, D.C.: The Brookings Institution.

Pressman, J., and A. Wildavsky. 1983. *Implementation.* 3rd ed. Berkeley and Los Angeles: University of California Press.

Reagan, M. 1987. *Regulation: The Politics of Policy.* Boston: Little, Brown and Co.

Redford, E. 1969. *Democracy in the Administrative State.* New York: Oxford University Press.

Rein, M., and F. Rabinovitz. 1978. "Implementation: A Theoretical Perspective." In *American Politics and Public Policy,* ed. W. Burnham and M. Weinberg, pp. 307–35. Cambridge, Mass.: MIT Press.

Ridgeway, V. F. 1983. "Dysfunctional Consequences of Performance Measurements." In *Readings in Public Administration,* 4th ed., ed. R. Golembiewski and F. Gibson, pp. 357–62. Boston: Houghton Mifflin Company.

Riker, W. 1964. *Federalism: Origin, Operation, Significance.* Boston: Little, Brown and Co.

Ripley, R., and G. Franklin. 1982. *Bureaucracy and Policy Implementation.* Homewood, Ill.: Dorsey Press.

Rivlin, A. 1971. *Systematic Thinking for Social Action.* Washington, D.C.: The Brookings Institution.

Rosenbaum, W. 1987. *Energy, Politics, and Public Policy.* Washington, D.C.: Congressional Quarterly Press.

Rossiter, C. 1961. *The Federalist Papers.* New York: The New American Library Inc.

Sabatier, P. 1986. "Top-Down and Bottom-Up Approaches to Implementation Research." *Journal of Public Policy* 6 (1): 21–48.

Sabatier, P., and D. Mazmanian. 1983. "The Conditions of Effective Implementation: A Guide to Accomplishing Policy Objectives." In *Readings in Public Administration,* ed. F. Nigro and L. Nigro, pp. 93–107. New York: Harper & Row.

Salamon, L. 1981. "Rethinking Public Management: Third-Party Government and the Changing Forms of Government Action." *Public Policy* 29 (3): 255–75.

Savas, E. S. 1987. *Privatization: The Key to Better Government.* Chatham, N.J.: Chatham House Publishers.

Schelling, T. 1970. *The Strategy of Conflict.* London: Oxford University Press.

Seidman, H. 1976. *Politics, Position, and Power.* New York: Oxford University Press.

Selznick, P. 1957. *Leadership in Administration.* New York: Harper & Row.

Senate, Select Committee on Nutrition and Human Needs. 1972. "Hunger in the Classroom: Then and Now." Washington, D.C.: Government Printing Office.

Senate, Committee on the Budget. 1981. "Omnibus Reconciliation Act of 1981." Washington, D.C.: Government Printing Office.

Sharp, E. 1981. "Models of Implementation and Policy Evaluation: Choice and its Implications." In *Implementing Public Policy,* ed. D. Palumbo and M. Harder, pp. 99–115. Lexington, Mass.: Lexington Books.

Slovic, P. 1987. "Perception of Risk." *Science* 236 (April 10, 1987: 280–85.

Steele, K. 1989. "Hanford: America's Nuclear Graveyard." *The Bulletin of the Atomic Scientists* 45 (8): 15–23.

———. 1988. "Hanford's Bitter Legacy." *The Bulletin of the Atomic Scientists* 44 (1): 17–23.

Stoker, R. 1989. "A Regime Framework for Implementation Analysis: Cooperation and Reconciliation of Federalist Imperatives." *Policy Studies Review* 9 (1): 29–49.

———. 1987. "Baltimore: The Self-Evaluating City?" In *The Politics of Urban Development,* ed. C. Stone and H. Sanders, pp. 244–66. Lawrence, Kan.: University Press of Kansas.

Stone, C. 1989. *Regime Politics: Governing Atlanta 1946–1988.* Lawrence, Kan.: University Press of Kansas.

———. 1987. "Summing Up: Urban Regimes, Development Policy, and Political Arrangements." In *The Politics of Urban Development,* ed. C. Stone and H. Sanders, pp. 269–90. Lawrence, Kan.: University Press of Kansas.

———. 1980. "The Implementation of Social Programs: Two Perspectives." *Journal of Social Issues* 36 (4): 13–34.

Stone, C., and H. Sanders, eds. 1987. *The Politics of Urban Development.* Lawrence, Kan.: University Press of Kansas.

Thompson, F. 1984. "Policy Implementation and Overhead Control."
     In *Public Policy Implementation,* ed. G. Edwards, pp. 3–26.
     Greenwich, Conn.: JAI Press.
Thompson, J. 1967. *Organizations in Action.* New York: McGraw Hill.
Van Horn, C., and D. Van Meter. 1976. "The Implementation of In-
     tergovernmental Policy." In *Public Policy Making in a Federal
     System,* ed. C. Jones and R. Thomas, pp. 39–62. Beverly Hills,
     Calif.: Sage Publications.
Walker, J. 1983. "The Origins and Maintenance of Group Interests in
     America." *American Political Science Review* 77 (2): pp. 390–406.
Weikart, D., and B. Banet. 1976. "Planned Variation from the Per-
     spective of a Model Sponsor." In *Social Program Implementation,*
     ed. W. Williams and R. Elmore, pp. 125–48. New York: Aca-
     demic Press.
Williams, W., ed. 1982. *Studying Implementation.* Chatham, N.J.:
     Chatham House.
Williams, W., and R. Elmore, eds. 1976. *Social Program Implementa-
     tion.* New York: Academic Press.
Yoder, K. 1987. "Low-level Rad Waste Seeks Home." *Pollution Engi-
     neering* 19 (11): 49–51.
Young, O. 1982. "Regime Dynamics: The Rise and Fall of International
     Regimes." *International Organization* 36 (2): 277–98.
———. 1980. "International Regimes: Problems of Concept Forma-
     tion." *World Politics* 32 (3): 331–56.

INDEX

Agencies, 119–21
Aid to Families with Dependent
  Children (AFDC), 104
ARIMA models, 142, 151
Atomic Energy Act of 1954, 154
Atomic Energy Commission, 154
Atomic waste. *See* Nuclear waste
Attractive partners, 91–92, 119–20
Authority, 3, 5, 6, 24, 25, 98, 188;
  diffuse, 14, 29, 34, 46–49, 120,
  178, 184, 187; shared, 11. *See
  also* Partnership
Authority paradigm, 22, 34, 39, 44,
  78, 94–95; and bureaucracy, 22;
  normative foundation of, 30; and
  implementation, 31–34
Axelrod, Robert, 62, 69, 72, 74, 80

Bank of Horton (Kan.), 122
Bardach, Eugene, 29, 46
Benda, P., 117
Berkovitz, Dan, 159–60
Block grants, 101
Bureaucracy, 27, 34, 142
Bureaucratic regime, 94, 96–100,
  186; coercive authority in, 98–99;
  cooperation in, 96; efficiency of,
  97; and nuclear waste, 165–66;
  IRS as example of, 97–100; limits
  of scope of, 100; popular control
  of, 166
Burnley, James IV, 109
Bush, George, 109

Chernobyl. *See* Nuclear accidents

Chicken Game, 70–72, 86
Civil Rights Act of 1964, 69
Clean Air Act, 111
Coldspring. *See* New town develop-
  ments
Commerce, 162
Commodity Credit Corporation,
  130, 132, 134–35, 138
Community Development Block
  Grants (CDBGs), 114–15
Compacting states, 160, 162
Complexity, 11, 81–82, 180–81
Compliance, 38–39
Compound majorities, 45, 178–79
Conflict of interest, 62–64
Conflict resolution, 50, 52, 61
Cooperation: and authority, 10, 23;
  and coercion, 58; conflicts of, 50,
  62–64, 177; defined, 61; encour-
  agement of, 54–55, 179, 186;
  exchange, 35; and the federal
  system, 9; and implementation
  process, 83–85; interstate, 163;
  and NSLP, 149; and nuclear
  waste, 163; ordering of, 21; and
  policy design, 183; and tacit bargaining, 73; versus compliance,
  182
Cooptation, 38
Corporate Average Fuel Economy
  (CAFE), 108–10
Corporate regimes, 96, 113–14, 115

Daley, Lawrence, 115

Deadlock, 40, 50, 61, 76, 161, 164, 174
Dean, James, 70
Department of Energy (DOE), 154, 157, 159, 166–70
Department of Transportation (DOT), 108
Derthick, Martha, 6, 7, 9, 46, 80
Disability thesis, 5, 13–14, 50, 169, 177; and exchange paradigm, 43; Hayek's restatement of, 48; and implementation paradox, 14–15; in nuclear waste, 169–70
District of Columbia, 11
Dominant strategy, 66, 70, 171
Donahue, John, 117–19
Downs, Anthony, 32
Dresang, D., 111

Economic Development Administration (EDA), 75–81
Education for All Handicapped Children Act (1975), 106
Elazar, Daniel, 5, 9, 11, 46, 49, 180
Employment Plan Review Board, 78
Energy Policy and Conservation Act of 1975, 108
Energy Reorganization Act, 154
Environmental Protection Agency (EPA), 108–13, 155
Etzioni, Amitai, 23
Exchange, 21, 40, 54–55, 81
Exchange paradigm, 34, 39–40, 44, 60, 78, 149; and implementation failure, 42–43; and public decisions, 42, 44; scope of, 42
Exit option, 104

Federalism, 3, 5, 10, 149, 177; cooperative, 41, 54; and governance, 5, 180; at its worst, 169–70
Federalist regime, 95, 100–04, 160, 165; and competition, 103–04;

design considerations of, 101; goal flexibility of, 101–02
Food and Drug Administration (FDA), 108
Food and Nutrition Service (USDA), 129
Ford Motor Company, 110
Formula grants, 101
Fort Lincoln. See New town developments
Free ride, 98

General Accounting Office (GAO), 130, 135, 167
Gentrification, 7
Gosling, J., 111
Governance: abilities of, 16; and concurrent jurisdictions, 45; costs of, 152–53; and diffuse authority, 49; noncentralized, 10; principles of, in U.S., 10–14; process of, 182
Grace Commission, The, 116
Gromley, William, 186
Guaranteed Student Loan Program, 124

Hamilton, Alexander, 54
Hanford, Wash., 170
Hardin, Garrett, 54, 68
Harmony, 40, 50, 61–62, 76
Hayek, F. A., 5, 12, 21, 47–50, 56
Henig, Jeffrey, 6, 115, 125
Higher Education Assistance Fund, 122
Hiskes, A., 155
Hiskes, R., 155
Hortatory controls, 186–87
Housing Act of 1949, 7
Housing and Community Development Act of 1974, 125

Implementation: aspects of, 4, 17; bottom-up approaches of, 17; and capacity to act, 16; and exchange

relationships, 20, 36, 37; and
governance, 48; as insulated from
scrutiny, 180; and performance
standards, 30, 33; politics of, 126;
process of, 25, 26, 31; programmed, 30, 182; problems of,
17, 20, 26, 36, 44, 183; task of,
17; top-down approaches of, 17
Implementation paradox, 4, 14, 31,
40, 49, 51, 177
Implementation participants, 4, 22,
28–29, 31, 91–93
Implementation regime, 90; creation
of, 57–58; defined, 55; design of,
93; development of, 84; and oversight, 186; typology of, 93–96
Implementation regime framework,
18, 53, 79, 149–50; and longitudinal research design, 88; and
policy design, 183–85; relationship of to international cooperation, 56–57; and exchange
paradigm, 60
Incentives. See Strategic context
Income tax, 98
Ingram, Helen, 46
Institutional context, 53, 174, 185
Interdependence, 26–27, 37–39
Internal Revenue Service (IRS), 97–
100
Interorganizational relations, 28
Issue linkage, 54, 74, 80–81, 150

Johnson, Lyndon B., 6–8, 46
Joint Committee on Atomic Energy,
154

Keohane, Robert, 61

Leadership, 3, 187
Leviathan, 68
Levine, C., 117
Liberalism, 3, 5, 12, 177
Lindblom, Charles, 6, 10, 21, 32, 35

Linder, S., 46
Low-level Radioactive Waste Policy
Act of 1980, 157, 161, 163–64

MacPherson, Craig, 122
Majority factions, 46. See also Com-
pound majorities
McLaughlin, Milbrey, 39
Military-industrial complex, 123
Miller, Robert, 173
Mixed motive context. See Mixed
motive interaction
Mixed motive game. See Mixed mo-
tive interaction
Mixed motive interaction, 40, 43,
54, 60–61, 76, 184; conditions re-
quired for, 61–62; types of, 64–
70; as analog to redistributive
programs, 85–86
Mixed motive strategic context. See
Mixed motive interaction
Monitored retrievable storage
(MRS) facility, 168
Montage, Charles, 175
Mutual adaptation, 38–40

National Conference of State Legislatures, 159
National Environmental Policy Act,
155
National Governors Association,
159
National School Lunch Act, 128
National School Lunch Program
(NSLP), 19, 127–51, 180; accountability in, 141–42; controversy concerning, 136–38; in
Ohio, 140–42; and partnership,
128; phases of, 131–36, 138–40,
142; and program reform, 142–
49; and section 11 participation,
129, 134–35
Nelson, Richard, 18
Nevada, 11, 157, 168–69

New Mexico, 157
New town developments: Coldspring, 114; Fort Lincoln, 8–9, 11,
   13, 15, 57–58, 80, 104
Nuclear accidents, 156
Nuclear Regulatory Commission,
   154, 158
Nuclear scandals, 166
Nuclear waste, 153–76; facilities for,
   164, 166, 168, 171–72; federal
   responsibility for, 164–65; high-
   level, 155–56, 164, 165; low-
   level, 155–56, 158–59, 160, 162,
   185; state responsibility for, 174;
   U.S. policy on, 157
Nuclear Waste Policy Act of 1982,
   111, 155, 157–58, 165–67, 173,
   175

Office of Seabed Research, 168
Old Age, Survivors, and Disability
   Insurance (OASDI), 98
Olson, Mancur, 54, 98
Omnibus Budget Reconciliation Act
   of 1981, 139–40
Organization, 21–22
Ostrom, Vincent, 45–47, 49, 54,
   179
Overhead democracy, 29–30
Oye, Kenneth, 68–69

Partial preemption, 111
Partnership, 10, 93, 128, 185–86.
   See also Authority
Pennsylvania, 156, 175
Peters, B. Guy, 46
Peterson, Paul, 114
Pluralism, 105
Pluralist regimes, 95, 105–06
Policy, 34–36, 59–60, 93, 183, 187.
   See also Program reform
Policy reform. See Program reform
Port of Oakland, Calif., 77

Power: coercive, 23, 57–59; normative, 23; as a paradox, 91; political, 15, 16, 48, 178; relationship
   to position, 91–93, 184–85; remunerative, 23–24
President's Commission on Regulatory Relief, 109
Pressman, J., 75–81
Prisoner's Dilemma, 65–68, 70, 86,
   161, 164
Privatization, 116–23; and accountability, 121–22; agency relationship in, 119–20; and competition,
   121, 123; definitions of, 116–17;
   efficiency of, 117–18; of nuclear
   waste disposal, 175–76; relevance
   of, to regime design, 119–20. See
   also Privatized regimes
Privatized regimes, 121–22
Program reform, 86–87, 180, 186;
   in lunch program, 142–49; as issue linkage, 150

Quasi market regimes, 96, 116,
   123–25; shared, 96, 125–26. See
   also Privatization

Rabe, B., 85–87
Reagan, Michael, 107, 111
Reagan, Ronald, 48, 108
Rebel Without a Cause, 70
Reciprocity, 35
Reform dilemma, 87–88
Reform strategy. See Program re-
   form
Regime analysis. See Implementa-
   tion regime framework; Regimes
Regime development, 80–89, 186.
   See also Implementation regime
   framework; Regimes
Regime framework. See Implemen-
   tation regime framework; Re-
   gimes

Regimes. *See* Corporate regimes; Pluralist regimes; Privatized regimes; Regulatory regimes
Regulatory regimes, 95–96, 106–10; shared 96, 107. *See also* Regimes
Reluctant partners, 33, 41, 51, 123; defined, 4; and mixed motive game, 61; power of, 46, 50
Reverse twist, 111
Rewards, 54
Ridgeway, V. F., 120
Rogers, Will, 97
Rosenbaum, Walter, 154, 169
Rothschild, Wis., 111
Rules of conduct. *See* Standards of conduct; Hortatory controls

SAS/ETS (statistical software package), 151
Savanah River Nuclear Facility, 158
Savas, E. S., 116–17
Section 8 Housing (Existing Housing Program), 125
Seidman, Harold, 91–92
Selznick, Philip, 21
Shadow government, 114–15
Skinner, Samuel, 109
Social safety net, 139
South Carolina, 157
Spontaneous order, 27, 57, 95
Stag Hunt, 68–69, 86
Stagnation, 39
Standards of conduct, 54, 74–75, 81, 186. *See also* Hortatory controls
State Planning Council on Radioactive Waste Management, 159
Steele, Karen, 170
Stone, Clarence, 15, 92, 114, 126
Strategic behavior, 28–29, 53
Strategic context, 53, 174, 183–85; in decisions to cooperate, 50; and nuclear waste, 160–63, 171–73

Subgovernments, 181

Tacit bargaining, 72–73
Thompson, James, 26
Three Mile Island. *See* Nuclear accidents
Tit-for-Tat, 72–73
Tragedy of the Commons, 54, 67

U.S. Circuit Court of Appeals, 11, 173
U.S. Department of Agriculture (USDA), 129–30, 136
U.S. Department of Health, Education, and Welfare (HEW), 135
U.S. Department of Housing and Urban Development (HUD), 8, 114, 125
U.S. Department of Justice, 173
U.S. government, 3, 5–6, 9–13, 45. *See also* Disability thesis
U.S. House of Representatives, Education and Labor Committee, 130
U.S. Senate, Select Committee on Nutrition and Human Needs, 130

Washington (state), 157
Washington, D.C. *See* District of Columbia
Waste Isolation Pilot Project (WIPP), 154–55, 157
Watkins, James, 173
Weyerhauser Paper Company, 111–13
Wildavsky, A., 75–81
Wong, K., 85–87
Working poor, 98
World Airways, 75–81

Young, Oran, 56, 60
Yucca Mountain, Nev., 11, 168–70, 173

Pitt Series in Policy and Institutional Studies
Bert A. Rockman, Editor

The Acid Rain Controversy
James L. Regens and Robert W. Rycroft

Affirmative Action at Work: Law, Politics, and Ethics
Bron Raymond Taylor

Agency Merger and Bureaucratic Redesign
Karen M. Hult

The Aging: A Guide to Public Policy
Bennett M. Rich and Martha Baum

Arms for the Horn: U.S. Security Policy in Ethiopia and Somalia, 1953–1991
Jeffrey A. Lefebvre

The Atlantic Alliance and the Middle East
Joseph I. Coffey and Gianni Bonvicini, Editors

The Budget-Maximizing Bureaucrat: Appraisals and Evidence
André Blais and Stéphane Dion, Editors

Clean Air: The Policies and Politics of Pollution Control
Charles O. Jones

The Competitive City: The Political Economy of Suburbia
Mark Schneider

Conflict and Rhetoric in French Policymaking
Frank R. Baumgartner

Congress and Economic Policymaking
Darrell M. West

Congress Oversees the Bureaucracy: Studies in Legislative Supervision
Morris S. Ogul

Democracy in Japan
Takeshi Ishida and Ellis S. Krauss, Editors

Demographic Change and the American Future
R. Scott Fosler, William Alonso, Jack A. Meyer, and Rosemary Kern

Economic Decline and Political Change: Canada, Great Britain, and the United States
Harold D. Clarke, Marianne C. Stewart, and Gary Zuk, Editors

Executive Leadership in Anglo-American Systems
Colin Campbell, S.J., and Margaret Jane Wyszomirski, Editors

Extraordinary Measures: The Exercise of Prerogative Powers in the United States
Daniel P. Franklin

Foreign Policy Motivation: A General Theory and a Case Study
Richard W. Cottam

"He Shall Not Pass This Way Again": The Legacy of Justice William O. Douglas
Stephen L. Wasby, Editor

Homeward Bound: Explaining Changes in Congressional Behavior
Glenn Parker

How Does Social Science Work? Reflections on Practice
Paul Diesing

Imagery and Ideology in U.S. Policy Toward Libya, 1969–1982
Mahmoud G. ElWarfally

The Impact of Policy Analysis
James M. Rogers

Iran and the United States: A Cold War Case Study
Richard W. Cottam

Japanese Prefectures and Policymaking
Steven R. Reed

Making Regulatory Policy
Keith Hawkins and John M. Thomas, Editors

Managing the Presidency: Carter, Reagan, and the Search for Executive Harmony
Colin Campbell, S.J.

Organizing Governance, Governing Organizations
Colin Campbell, S.J., and B. Guy Peters, Editors

Party Organizations in American Politics
Cornelius P. Cotter et al.

Perceptions and Behavior in Soviet Foreign Policy
Richard K. Herrmann

Pesticides and Politics: The Life Cycle of a Public Issue
Christopher J. Bosso

Policy Analysis by Design
Davis B. Bobrow and John S. Dryzek

The Political Failure of Employment Policy, 1945–1982
Gary Mucciaroni

Political Leadership: A Source Book
Barbara Kellerman, Editor

The Politics of Public Utility Regulation
William T. Gormley, Jr.

The Politics of the U.S. Cabinet: Representation in the Executive Branch, 1789–1984
Jeffrey E. Cohen

The Presidency and Public Policy Making
George C. Edwards III, Steven A. Shull, and Norman C. Thomas, Editors

Private Markets and Public Intervention: A Primer for Policy Designer
Harvey Averch

Public Policy in Latin America: A Comparative Survey
John W. Sloan

Reluctant Partners: Implementing Federal Policy
Robert P. Stoker

Roads to Reason: Transportation, Administration, and Rationality in Colombia
Richard E. Hartwig

Site Unseen: The Politics of Siting a Nuclear Waste Repository
Gerald Jacob

The Struggle for Social Security, 1900–1935
Roy Lubove

Tage Erlander: Serving the Welfare State, 1946–1969
Olof Ruin

Traffic Safety Reform in the United States and Great Britain
Jerome S. Legge, Jr.

Urban Alternatives: Public and Private Markets in the Provision of Local Services
Robert M. Stein

The U.S. Experiment in Social Medicine: The Community Health Center Program, 1965–1986
Alice Sardell